AF333322

Baby Boom
Memories

Baby Boom Memories

James Murphy

Tresanton Publishing
Charlotte, North Carolina

Baby Boom Memories

by James Murphy

Published by:

Tresanton Publishing
Post Office Box 472847
Charlotte, North Carolina 28247-2847 U.S.A.

ISBN 0-9658833-5-3

Library of Congress Catalog Number 97-90731

Contents

Contents

Chapter One

1957–1958

Kathleen, Rubber Shoes and The Yankees

New Haven, Connecticut is a city on Long Island Sound. I was born there on October 23, 1952. I have a brief memory here and there, but can't really put a time on things until I entered kindergarten at the age of four in September 1957. Up to that point, my life consisted of Mom, Dad and my brother, Howie, who was almost four years older than me.

We lived in a six-room Cape Cod style house with an attached garage in one of New Haven's suburbs, Hamden. Most of the families were like mine: they would eventually have two to five kids, all of whom would be known as "Baby Boomers" years later. It seemed that the families around Furman Road were mostly Irish, Italian and Jewish. In the fall of 1957 most families had one car, and the mothers were home with the kids.

Howie was starting the fourth grade at the parochial school, Saint John the Baptist. They did not have kindergarten there, so I went to the public school about a half a mile away from home: Helen Street School. Kindergarten students went for half days. Mrs. Miller was my teacher. My friend from across the street, Billy Garcia (pronounced Gar-sha), also started school, but he was in the other class. I think his teacher was called Miss Duponte.

I only remember a couple of kids in my class, a very cute girl with short dark hair and bangs named Kathleen and a rather loud boy named Jacky. I didn't like Jacky too much because he got to walk to recess every day next to Kathleen, holding her hand. My partner was not nearly as pretty, I think his name was Dennis.

One day, we were going outside for recess to play *Hokey Pokey* and Jacky was absent. I was able to move up one spot in line and walk with Kathleen, something I liked very much. That night, I think I mentioned to my family how I hoped Jacky would be sick for a long time. I remember a long lecture following that comment. Something about that kind of thought normally being a *sin,* but I wasn't seven years old yet, so I couldn't actually have any sins for a couple of more years. Anyway, it turned out I didn't need to get off on that technicality. Jacky was back in school the next day and I was off the hook.

I hated having to wear a stupid pair of black rubbers any time it rained. It's not that I had anything against keeping my feet dry, but it was an incredible hassle trying to get those tight things on and off. They were too small!

One rainy afternoon, we were getting ready to go home. Mrs. Miller told me to put on these rubbers from hell. Naturally, I expected her to assist me and was appalled when she said I was old enough to do it myself. We had quite an argument as the rest of the class was leaving. I finally surrendered and, through my tears, started to stretch those stupid black rubbers over my big shoes. I worked and worked. My fingers were on the verge of bleeding (so I thought). Somehow, I was able to get one rubber securely on. I waited for all the praise and encouragement from Mrs. Miller, but she simply said, "Now the other one."

By this time, I'll bet five minutes had passed since the other kids left, and I was in no mood to go through that effort again with another stupid rubber. I jumped up, one rubber on my foot, the other in my hand, yelled at her and tore out of the class crying all the way. Somehow I made it home and was able to get the one rubber off my foot before I went inside. As far as Mom was concerned, all was well with her good little boy, Jimmy. The next day, Mrs. Miller never even brought it up. It turned out to be one of the very few times in my life I misbehaved outside the home and didn't get caught.

That winter, my family was preparing for the arrival of a new baby. Mom was making a trip to St. Raphael's Hospital in New Haven for a few days. Grandma Vivian was going to stay with us, which was the best news I could get. She was my pal, and any visit from Grandma was a treat. She explained to me that God makes babies appear at hospitals just in case they might need a doctor. Made sense to me!

On Valentine's Day, 1958, Maureen Murphy was born and was expected to come home a few days later. My father must have taken some time off from work, because he was waiting for me when I marched out of kindergarten later that week. I hollered to him across the street, "Hey Dad, how's the baby?" He told me she was fine, and she was now home, waiting to see her big brother. He also explained to me in the car how I was going to have to be very gentle with my new sister.

I remember getting home and running into the room where she was sleeping in a little crib. I was somewhat worried about her color, but no one else seemed to notice. I hated to put a damper on everyone's fun, but she appeared to me to be quite reddish. She probably had a little rash or something, but when Mom, Dad and Grandma asked me how I liked my baby sister, I had to be honest. I stared into the crib and said, "I like her, but why did you have to get an Indian?"

Second only to the excitement of getting a new Indian was going to a major league baseball game. Yankee Stadium to a five year old boy had to be one of the greatest places on earth. In the summer of 1958, Dad took Howie, Grandpa Vivian, Uncle Phil, Howard Kunemund (Grandpa's cousin) and me to a ball game. This was the original stadium, not the one refurbished in the 1970s.

It was a different time: the four grownups wore jackets and ties with hats. The family car was washed for the occasion. We were driving to New York City!

Before we entered the ballpark, we went across the street under some train tracks for lunch. We ate at a little deli that had baked ham piled high on a sandwich. I never had a better meal!

I still remember the excitement of finishing our wonderful sandwiches and milkshakes, crossing back under the *El* toward the ballpark. The smell of cigars outside went hand in hand with the cooking of the pretzels. There seemed to be thousands of people milling about.

Walking through the tunnel and seeing the light at the end made the anticipation incredible, and I was not to be disappointed. I will never forget how we came out of that darkness and into a different world: the greenest grass I had ever seen, bright blue sky, tens of thousands of people everywhere, and vast, vast space. It was overwhelming. I don't think I ever actually noticed the outfield fence, but somehow believed you had to hit the ball over the bleachers for a homer.

Then, of course, there were the Yankees down there, going through their batting practice, bright white uniforms, pinstripes and numbers. Howie kept pointing out Number 7: Mickey Mantle was taking his swings. We were seated behind third base, and I watched him batting left handed, ripping line drives into the right field seats. The crack of his bat echoed through the stadium and the crowd would cheer on every swing. Dad noticed how players from both teams were crowded around the batting cage watching him, learning from him.

I can't recall who the Yankees played that day, or who even won the game. However, I do remember the drive back to Connecticut that night, the guys around me, wishing my day was just beginning again.

Chapter Two

1958–1959

The Nuns and "Buck-Buck"

I moved up to the big school in the fall of 1958, first grade at Saint John the Baptist. Back then, school always opened up on the Wednesday after Labor Day. We also went with half days that Wednesday, Thursday and Friday. I guess they figured it was easier for the kids to ease into the school year that way.

Saint John's was to become a big part of my life for the next eight years. This was where I was to attend school and learn the ways of the Church. The school was a two-story brick building, enormous in my eyes. It was located on a busy road on the border of New Haven and Hamden, just on the New Haven side, called Dixwell Avenue. A smaller street, Elizabeth Street, ran off of Dixwell, separating the school and school yard from the church, convent and rectory.

On the first day of school, I remember seeing six hundred kids wandering around the school yard, waiting for the opening bell to call us inside. Here and there, towering above this mass of humanity, roamed about ten or twelve nuns. Not only were they the only obvious grown-ups in the schoolyard, but they were easily identified by the black habits and the starched white head-dresses. These head-dresses were unbelievable. They squeezed the face together, had some starched contraption going from the chin down their chest, and finally, a very sharp starched point soaring into the air about six inches over their forehead. I don't think I had ever seen anything quite like it. Most of them didn't seem to look very happy, either, and I didn't know why. All I knew was these people were not to be taken lightly. I was going to be a good boy.

I noticed one little girl crying her eyes out while one of the Sisters was comforting her. It turns out her name was Patricia, and she would be in my class.

At Saint John's, each grade had two classes, 1A and 1B, 2A and 2B, etc. I was in 1B and my teacher was Mother Saint Sean. She could have been 25 years old or 65 years old; I had no idea with that outfit. However, by the end of that first day, I wasn't as afraid of nuns. Mother Saint Sean turned out to be a lovely lady, very gentle and very patient.

I learned how to sound out words and slowly how to read. I recall one word giving me lots of trouble for a couple of days, *any*. I would think that word should be spelled *e-n-y*. I kept trying to sound it out and I wanted to use the small *a* sound, as in *apple*. It just didn't make sense.

Early in that school year, Mother Saint Sean told us that she would be announcing the winners of the Dominic

Savio pins. I guess whoever acted like this saint would get a pin, which was about the size of a quarter, with a couple of purple ribbons hanging from it. Naturally, I assumed I would be getting one. It was just a matter of who my fellow Dominic Savio club members would be.

That Friday she began handing the pins out. I waited. She handed out some more. I waited. She said she had one more. I held my breath. She announced the name of Thomas Smith. I cried. Mother Saint Sean came over and asked me what was wrong. I cried more. The kids were all staring. I mumbled something about wanting to be in the Dominic Savio Club. Somehow she got her hands on one more pin. I was in. Lesson to be learned: None, because I don't think I ever got anything else by crying.

We lived for recess and lunch. School probably went from 8:45 a.m. to 2:45 p.m. At 10:30, our class was able to go outside for about fifteen minutes. Almost from day one, I had a few friends who played football every morning recess with me. We had a little brown *pixie football* which was perfect for touch games. It was always three against three. My team consisted of Jimmy Reardon, Joey Tyler and me. We went up against Robert Caron, Thomas Smith and Frederick Starno. We did this for all eight years. It was total razzle-dazzle, and every other play was a *bomb*.

The worst sound in the morning was the schoolyard bell going off to call us inside when recess was over. Actually, it was two bells, the first one was to *freeze* us, the second one, about four seconds later, was to get us going to our *line*. We would form two lines, smallest people in front, one for the boys and one for the girls.

We would wait for the nuns to march us back into the school. Once we got back in, it was just a matter of time before we would look forward to lunch.

Lunch hour was interesting. It began at 11:45 and went to 12:45. Some of the kids went home for lunch, but most of us had to eat in the lunchroom. Four hundred of us filed into the lunchroom, said a few prayers, and settled into our brown paper bags and lunch boxes. Each person also got a carton of white milk, which cost five cents.

The strange thing was that we were not allowed to talk while we ate. We were supposed to sit in absolute silence. The penalty for talking was having to stand up *against the wall.* While everyone else was enjoying their peanut butter and jelly sandwiches, the accused had to wait for lunch to be over. Then, as each class was called out to recess (eighth grade first, down to the first grade), you got to walk by the *bad* kids who were against the wall. They were the last ones to go outside. I don't remember ever seeing a girl up there. It was always the same few boys and sometimes a new face. I had to stand up against the wall twice in my eight years.

Lunch was over in twenty minutes, but the recess that followed was forty minutes. With all 600 children running around, it was different than morning recess. The boys all seemed to be *shooting* baseball cards in the spring. There was a sort of curb that bordered one side of the schoolyard. You played against another boy by shooting cards against .the curb, the closest one to the curb was the winner, and the winning boy kept both cards. Basically, it was a form of gambling, but no one seemed to mind. Sometimes, you constructed a specific *shooter,* made out of roof tiles you found around the schoolyard. Then, if you lost, you'd give a baseball card to the winner. You never wagered a *good* card, which was a Yankee or a famous player from another team. Usually, you tried to find a smaller kid and get as much as you could from him.

A crack ran down the schoolyard, and the boys were supposed to stay on one side, the girls on the other. Probably 70% of the yard was for the boys, 30% for the girls. The girls usually spent their time jumping rope or hitting hands and reciting something about a *girl dressed in black, black, black.*

The boys who weren't shooting baseball cards were usually playing *buck-buck, white horse* or *ring-a-lario.* With all the people milling about during the noon hour recess, you were supposed to be a little more calm as opposed to the morning recess. One time, Mother Saint Laura grabbed me while I was running by and asked me, "Mister Murphy, how many times have I told you not to run wildly during the lunch recess?" She seemed to be waiting for an answer, and I didn't realize that there was no proper response, but I thought about the question carefully and answered, "seven?" I guess it was a pretty good answer because she let me go with a warning.

Every month we had something called First Friday at the church. Each class would march over from the school to the church at 11:00 a.m. The first graders were in the front of the church in pews going all the way back to the eighth graders. Saint John the Baptist had a beautiful altar, all in white marble. The paintings and statues of Jesus, Mary, and the saints were gorgeous, too, and the Stations of the Cross were almost life-like. I'll never forget the first time I heard the whole school sing a hymn called *Holy God We Praise Thy Name.* The second line says, "Lord of all, we bow before Thee." It was this line that gave me shivers. The older students were taught to sing a different melody than all the other kids, and a sort of rumbling rolled from the back of the church down to the front. I didn't realize at the time, but all that was happening was something called *harmony.* I never heard anything like it in my life. Boy, it sounded great. You really felt that you were close to heaven. I looked forward to First Friday every month just to hear that song.

Later in the school year, we learned about Lent, and we were able to get out of school at about 1:45 p.m. every Friday from Ash Wednesday to Easter to attend the Stations of the Cross. The pictures in our little red booklets were just bloody and graphic enough to keep our interest, and we were able to enjoy another treat, incense. The smell of that smoke creeping over the church was wonderful. Again, you felt that you were as close to heaven as you could get while still being alive.

I almost hated it when Easter came. If it weren't for the candy, it would have been quite a letdown. I was probably the only one who wanted Lent to continue for several more weeks. Even the purple robes on the priests looked so cool compared to the other colors.

Chapter Three

1959–1960

Confessions of a Second-Grader

I started second grade in the fall of 1959. Instead of a nun, I had a lay teacher named Mrs. Reilly. Saint John's probably had 14 nuns and four "civilians" back then. Someone had told me that she was really a rough teacher, but I remember her being pretty nice. Besides her, I only have a few memories of Class 2-B. One was a girl named Phyllis. I don't think she was in Saint John's after the second grade, but she made a big impression on me that year. She was probably the smartest one in the class, and the best looking, too, as far as I could see. I was lucky enough to sit right in front of her.

I also remember the steel bar that held my desk together. This was the first desk I had that didn't have a separate table and chair. This was one of those kinds where the table was attached to the chair, and you put your books underneath. That steel bar was a perfect place to get relief from the constant itching that I had on my wrists in the winter. When I played out in the snow for hours, my wet mittens or gloves created quite a rash around my wrists. They seemed to itch all the time, and I would rub them up against that steel bar in school all day long. Actually, I did it too hard and too often, because my skin would become so raw it would start to bleed.

It was about this time that my grandfather was getting sick. He had some kind of cancer and was at the hospital a couple of times. He and Grandma Vivian lived in Ansonia, Connecticut, about thirty minutes away from our house in Hamden. We spent every Saturday afternoon visiting them in Ansonia and every Sunday afternoon visiting Grandma Murphy in Derby, which was next to Ansonia.

Both places were part of an area in Connecticut called *The Valley*, a little collection of mill towns built near the Housatonic and Naugatuck Rivers. Both towns seemed very old, and of course, all the people we visited there were very old as well.

Saturday afternoon at Grandma and Grandpa Vivian's house wasn't too bad. They had a nice television and Coca Cola. There were also some boys for my brother and me to play games with in the neighborhood, usually baseball or football. The Sunday visit to Grandma Murphy's, however, was a lot more boring. There were really no kids to play with, no television, and no food that we were interested in. Most of the time we sat and listened to a bunch of gossip from ladies in their eighties.

On the weekend drives out to The Valley, I began to have occasional bouts of car sickness. More than once my father had to pull over so I could throw up out the back of the car. I guess I was having several stomach aches, too, and was taken to see our family physician, Doctor McKeon. Usually he made house calls, but this was an office visit.

We learned that I had an inflamed appendix, and I was going to have to have an operation, quickly. I remember having this explained to me when we got back home, being quite frightened and doing a lot of crying. I went to the hospital that same evening.

I got to Saint Raphael's Hospital and somehow I think we were still under the impression that they needed to do a few more tests to see if I really was going to need surgery. When I woke up the next morning in the hospital bed, I learned that I was going to be having the operation that day.

The nurses kept scolding me, because I kept putting my hands on my stomach after they had sterilized the area. I bet they had to do it over again at least four times. I also remember some other preparations that were pretty gross.

Well, I guess I came through the operation OK, but I will never forget the first time I tried to get up to go to the bathroom. I was not used to that kind of discomfort! I also had a huge bandage, and the surgeon came in and drew on it, a picture of how the cut and stitches looked. He did it with a ball-point pen so I was able to show anyone who visited.

Back then, you stayed in the hospital several days after this type of surgery. I was feeling all right after the second day and began to meet some of the other children on the floor. I think some of them had serious illnesses, and I can recall making a couple of good friends in those few days. One of the best nights in the hospital was watching a Walt Disney television show called *Moochie of the Little League*. I was feeling stronger, had my own television with my own controls, and my relatives were all around me. It was a great night!

When I left the hospital, I was going to get to stay out of school for two or three more weeks. There was a party at my house for my homecoming, and I was the center of attention. I remember going for a walk with Dad around the block in a bright red coat, moving rather slowly, trying to regain my strength. Many of the neighbors came out of their houses to speak to me and see how I was doing. That was a lot of fun.

I also received get well cards from all my classmates from 2B, a project they probably had to do in our Friday afternoon art class. I even got one from Phyllis, but the best one was from Thomas Smith. It showed a face with the eyes hanging out of their sockets by a string. It read, *My eyes are popping out for you.* That card was the coolest.

During my recuperation, Mom kept saying how lucky I was that I would be getting through all this well before it was time for First Holy Communion that spring. First Communion and First Confession were big deals, and we practiced and practiced to get ready for them. Unfortunately, just days before the big events, I came down with the chicken pox and had to miss being part of the festivities. I was going to have to make my First Confession and First Communion a week after my classmates.

Actually, having the chicken pox or any "big" illness was kind of fun. You got to stay out of school, lie on the couch and watch TV, and you were the star attraction. The ideal situation was having a high fever, because then you were too sick to be bored by lying on the couch. When you began to recover, you started to get more energy and began to get a little restless. Then, only the mornings were fun. All the good reruns were on. But in the afternoons, you were forced to watch Mom's *stories,* which were later known as soap operas. I thought they stunk.

Anyway, at the beginning of my week of chicken pox, I remember watching a Walt Disney show on a Sunday night. I usually did not care for the animated shows, or even the shows about nature. What I loved were the shows that related to American History. My favorites were *Davy Crockett, King of the Wild Frontier* and *Francis Marion, The Swamp Fox.*

That Sunday night I watched *The Swamp Fox* from the *sick couch* surrounded by my family, eating cinnamon toast Mom had made for me, and maybe a little Coca Cola to go along with it. It was a perfect night.

A couple of weeks later it was time for me to make my First Confession. Now remember, I had been *sinning* since the day I turned seven years old six or seven months earlier, so it was imperative that I got it all out on the table. I had a pretty good idea of what my sins were, but had trouble with the number of times I had committed each one. I hated to say I did something twenty-seven times if it turned out to be thirty. I figured if I got hit by a car and died after that confession, I might just miss getting into heaven since I forgot three of them. Therefore, I figured I should make my first confession with big numbers . . . better to be safe than sorry.

To make my First Confession, I was taken over to church one weekday morning. There were three priests: Father Frisbee, Father Kevin, and Monsignor Donnely, who was the boss. My favorite was Father Frisbee.

I walked into the confessional, knelt down in the darkness, and waited for the sound of the sliding wooden door that told me it was my turn. I had to wait a few minutes for Father Frisbee to wrap things up with the confessor on the other side and couldn't believe how long it was taking. That person must have had some serious mortal sins to talk about. Finally, I heard the door on my side slide open.

"Bless me Father for I have sinned. This is my first confession and these are my sins . . . I fought with my brother ten thousand times." (I heard a chuckle.) "I disobeyed my mother fifteen thousand times." (I heard more chuckling and some groaning, too.) "I disobeyed my father . . . once!" (That's when he lost it.) "I'm sorry for these sins and all the sins of my past life." Father Frisbee finally collected himself and said, "OK, Murph, for your penance say three *Hail Mary*s and one *Our Father*. Then he absolved me from all my sins. I was totally clean for at least an hour. It didn't last long, but it was a nice feeling.

Chapter Four

1960–1961
Funeral and Holidays

Istarted third grade in September 1960 under the guidance of a nun called Mother Saint Ellen Frances. She also had a reputation as being one of the tougher nuns in school, but I hit it off with her. In fact, I was competing with a girl for being number one in the class. Her name was Maureen Smith. This competition would continue until the sixth grade, when the Beatles came to America. Then I sort of fell into the middle of the pack.

That September things were a little bit different on Saturdays. Many of the trips out to Ansonia were not quite the same. Grandpa Vivian was sometimes there, sometimes not. He was in and out of the hospital. No one really explained to me what the problem was, but I knew it was pretty serious. Something else was happening about this time also. A hurricane or some large storm was threatening the area, and we had a day off from school. But I didn't enjoy it. Something was wrong. We learned later in the week through a phone call that Grandpa had passed away.

It was decided that I was going to be able to attend the wake and the funeral. I was going to be seeing a body! Howie and I spent a lot of time talking about this. He and I were pretty scared about it. The suspense was powerful walking into that funeral home, but it turned out not to be so scary. There were flowers everywhere, organ music in the background and a lot of people standing around talking. Grandpa looked fine, too. He just looked like he was sleeping. Everyone kept saying how he was already up in heaven. I spent a lot of time trying to figure out the mystery of dead bodies and live souls. I also wondered why our limousine could go through red lights on the way to the cemetery.

Luckily, I didn't have to attend too many funerals as a kid and could focus on the happier times—the holidays. Thanksgiving was one of my favorites. First of all, we saw the big parade on television in the morning. My family used to watch CBS, where Captain Kangaroo was the host from his *magic window.* The best part about the parade was when Santa Claus came down the street at the end. It meant that the big day was now in sight. Then it was out to Aunt Cha's and Uncle Phil's. Nothing smelled better than their house on Thanksgiving Day. The turkey always seemed to be twenty-three pounds, and we would be disappointed when occasionally it was twenty-one or twenty-two. Stuffing was always the best part of the meal. We would eat so much that Aunt Cha would not only fill the turkey, but make a bunch more as big loaves wrapped in aluminum foil.

Another fun thing each Thanksgiving was keeping the football game on while we had our dinner at 12:30 p.m. The Detroit Lions played every year at that time, and even though we were all New York Giants fans, the whole family had known one of the stars of the Lions since he was a kid. His name was Nick Pietrasante. He grew up across the street from where my parents had their first rental house in Ansonia.

Of course, the greatest holiday was Christmas. In our family, Christmas Eve was pretty big, too. We all went out to Aunt Cha's and Uncle Phil's where there was a large number of presents around the fake fireplace. Unfortunately, the presents were always clothes. The good stuff didn't come until Santa brought it. We had to wait until the next morning.

Once an eight-year-old is in bed on Christmas Eve, the next few hours may well be the most miserable of the year. First of all, you simply couldn't get into a deep sleep. The night would just go on and on forever. If you were lucky enough to drift off to sleep, it was only for a few minutes. You may have thought you had slept all night and it was just a matter of an hour or so before you could get up. You would lie there, guessing about the time. There were no lights on in my room, and I never thought about getting up and turning them on to see the time. There were certainly no digital clocks that lit up, either. I swear there were times when I actually believed the earth had stopped turning and we would never see daylight again.

When we finally could get up, the living room held presents for all of us. Some of my favorite ones over the years usually had something to do with little toy soldiers. Whether it was cowboys and Indians, WW II GIs, or my favorites, Civil War soldiers, I would be in heaven. I loved to set up huge battle scenes. I enjoyed that for years.

That winter, the third grade went on a field trip to downtown New Haven. There was a large religious convention going on. Every sort of Catholic clergy was there: bishops, monsignors, priests, brothers and nuns. Many of them represented missions from all over the world. You could sign up with any of the booths if you wanted to obtain more information on a certain religious life. I don't know what got into me, but I signed up for every possible thing I could and talked to every missionary I could. A few weeks later, I started to receive more stuff in the mail than you could imagine. My family was convinced I was to become a *great white father.*

Actually, I was getting pretty religious at this point in my life. I would spend hours reading a group of picture books called *The Crusades.* There were twenty or so separate booklets going from Adam and Eve and the rest of the Old Testament all the way up to the crucifixion of Jesus. The stories were absolutely fantastic! The pictures were terrific too. Lots of good fights, swords, blood, etc. Some of the best were: Cain killing Abel; David killing Goliath; David's son Absolem hanging in a tree by his long hair; and the head of John the Baptist on a plate.

Some of the best stories were Jacob and his brother Esau—Jacob trying to marry the good looking girl, Rachel, but getting tricked into marrying the plain girl, Leah. I always loved anything about Moses and the escape from Egypt. The Old Testament always had better stories as far as I was concerned. There was more fighting and violence. The New Testament was a little tame for an eight-year-old.

Between the missionaries and the Crusades, I was convinced I was going to be a priest. My new hobby was decorating my room and bureau with every possible religious artifact I could find. Aunt Cha's house was a treasure house for finding little statues and old rosary beads. This obsession may have lasted a month or so.

That year, the third and fourth graders were putting on a spring musical. There was a lot of dancing. Mother Saint Ellen Frances somehow knew how to waltz and taught several of us the basic box step. I was dancing with a girl named Barbara Robertson and we kind of took to it quickly. Instead of just doing the basic square moves, we could get up on our toes and make some pretty big circles. Mother Saint Ellen taught us a few twirls and something called a hesitation step. At one point in the show, we were going to do our own solo, with me in a tuxedo and Barbara in an evening gown.

After weeks of practice, we were ready for the big event. The school gymnasium was filled with parents, nuns and priests from all over the area. Barbara and I waited in the wings, poised for stardom in dancing to *The Blue Danube.* The music started and out we came. I knew we were great! The whole dance went off perfectly, without a hitch.

Unfortunately, when the song ended, we were supposed to walk elegantly from the middle of the stage to the very front holding hands and performing a very formal bow and curtsy. Barbara forgot this part, and when I took her hand which was enclosed in a long white glove, she froze. The glove slipped right off her hand and I walked elegantly to the front of the stage holding nothing but the long white glove. I took a long bow by myself to the laughter and roars of the audience. Oh well, so we weren't Fred Astaire and Ginger Rogers.

That spring and summer was the last season I was too young to play organized baseball. Our town didn't have a Little League, but we did have the Hamden Father's

Baseball Association, which was a fantastic baseball league. You had to be nine years old. I was always the bat boy on my brother's team, and my father was always an assistant coach. Howie and I were both good ball players, and I had a big advantage over the kids my age since I spent so much time playing with my brother and his friends, who were all four years older than me. Everybody thought I was going to be the next Mickey Mantle, but unfortunately, by the time I was twelve or thirteen, most of the other kids my age were starting to catch up to me.

That year I will always remember because there was another boy on Howie's team that had a younger sister, maybe a year or two older than me. Her name was Barbara Gotlieb. She had long dark hair and big dark eyes and she was absolutely gorgeous. I don't think I ever talked to her, but I do know I was head over heels in love. Any time she was at a baseball game, I could hardly keep my mind on my responsibilities - keeping the bats in order. Sometimes her hair was pulled up. Other times she wore a long pony tail. I couldn't believe the effect she had on me.

Later that summer, we went on our first real vacation to Cape Cod. We rented a cottage in a place called East Sandwich. This would be the beginning of three years in a row of going to Cape Cod for two weeks each summer. These were some of the best times of my life.

John Kennedy was our new President, Irish and Catholic, and my family and most of the teachers at school were huge fans of his. Much of our vacations centered around Kennedy watching. On Friday afternoon we would go over to Otis Air Force Base where we waited for Air Force 1 to arrive. President and Mrs. Kennedy would get off the plane, wave to the crowd, and board a helicopter to take them to Hyannis Port. On Sunday morning, after we attended Mass, we would run around to the back entrance of Saint Francis Xavier Church to wait for their limousine. They would pull up and walk right in front of us into the church. Then we would wait another hour for them to walk right in front of us out of the church. On Mondays, we would be back at Otis Air Force Base to say good-bye. It sounds a little crazy now. However, the last time we did this, the President came over to the crowd. He walked straight over to where I was standing, shook my hand and said, "How are you, son?" My family was standing near me and they couldn't believe it. What a thrill.

Actually, there was a lot more to the Cape Cod vacations than Kennedy watching. Most days started off with a good breakfast in the cottage followed by some whiffle ball in the backyard. Later in the morning, we would walk a few hundred yards up the street to the ocean. This was the northern part of Cape Cod, Cape Cod Bay. The water was ice cold there, but there were terrific sandbars we could play on.

One of our traditions was going to the little store each morning to buy a new comic book. They were ten cents back then. My favorites were *Superboy, Batman and Robin* and *Casper the Friendly Ghost.* My brother always liked the *Richie Rich* comic books. I especially liked any *Superboy* episodes where he went back into time. My favorite was when Superboy almost stopped John Wilkes Booth from assassinating President Lincoln at Ford's Theater.

Later on, we would return to the cottage for a good lunch. Then it would be off to Craigville Beach in Hyannis on the Nantucket Sound side of the Cape. The water was much warmer there, and there were pretty good waves. We would spend the afternoon swimming and body surfing.

Then it was back to the cottage to clean up and get ready for the evening. The nighttime was just as good as the daytime. We would drive into Hyannis, park the car and eat out at one of the restaurants on the main street. Usually, we would either go to a place called the Mayflower or another restaurant called the Blue Anchor. I always had a huge appetite after spending the day running around and swimming and could eat like any adult. Normally, I would order a hot roast turkey sandwich with stuffing or fried scallops.

After dinner, we would stroll down the main street to one of the nicest miniature golf courses around. I can still remember twelve of the eighteen holes. If you were lucky enough to get a hole in one on the last one you would get a free game. Then we would do some more walking, often stopping by the various artists doing their paintings or their chalk drawings on canvas. One time, my parents had an artist make a picture of Maureen. That was fun to watch.

The final event of the evening was heading toward the penny candy store, right next to a big clock on the main street. We were each given fifteen cents to do our shopping. We would grab the little baskets and begin to price out the candy, most of which was a penny a piece or three for a penny. It probably took us half an hour to get our fifteen cents worth.

Then it was off to the cottage, maybe an hour or so of TV watching and finally bedtime. As usual, Howie and I shared a room. Funny enough, as I settled into bed each night, I kept thinking that this part of the vacation was just as good as all the things we did during the day and evening. I was probably so worn out from all the activities that bed never felt better. Much of the time before I fell asleep was spent figuring out how many days we had left for our vacation. I hated when we were past the midpoint.

I also remember something that was very interesting to me. Every time we were at the beach, there were many helicopters, planes and even blimps moving over the water. Dad said they were looking out for submarines and small boats because President Kennedy's summer home was nearby. Many of the grownups, and certainly the newscasters on television, were often talking about the problems with Russia and Cuba.

Toward the end of the summer of '61, my father, Howie and I were keeping track of what was happening in baseball. Roger Maris, one of my beloved Yankees, was chasing Babe Ruth's record of sixty home runs in a single season. We followed that very closely. I remember his hitting number fifty nine and number sixty and it all coming down to the last day of the season, October 1. I'll never forget when he took that inside pitch and rifled it into the right field bleachers. Phil Rizzuto was the broadcaster, and his call of the action stayed with me forever. "Fast ball . . . Hit deep to right!! . . . This could be it . . . Way back there . . . Holy Cow . . . He did it! . . . Sixty one for Maris . . . Holy Cow! . . . What a shot! . . . Look at them fight for that ball out there! . . . Another standing ovation for Roger Maris." That was one of the most thrilling moments in sports for me. I also noticed that in the following spring, wearing Number Nine was almost as cool as wearing Number Seven in the baseball league.

Chapter Five

1961–1962

Running the Neighborhood

When school started in the fall of 1961, things were looking great for me. I had a lay teacher, Miss Grillo, who took a big liking to me. I was getting good grades and having a lot of fun at school each day.

During the summer, I hung around with the kids on my street, Furman Road. My best pals were Billy Garcia, Bonnie Lipton and Jimmy Zarro. However, they went to the public school, and I kind of lost contact with them during the school year. So from September until June, my best friend in the world was Jimmy Reardan, who lived three streets over from me on Michael Road. Jimmy had a knack for making whatever we did much more interesting than it should have been. For one thing, Jimmy fancied himself a real woodsman, and he and I spent countless hours down in the woods and swamps near our homes. He and I always seemed to be building some sort of fort, whether it was made from woodscraps or snow.

He also made Halloween one of the best nights of the year. Jimmy and I would make our plans a good week before the big event. We would map out the neighborhoods near us and come up with our strategies as to where we should go. The best neighborhoods were where the houses were closest together. Our parents would not let us go out until 6:00, but what we accomplished in two and a half hours was amazing. I would always wear the same red devil's costume year after year. I can still smell the plastic and sparkles on it. Every once in a while my mother humiliated me by making me go out on Halloween in that costume with a hat on because it was a little too cold. It was almost like wearing a big neon sign over my head flashing, "I am a complete nerd. Please beat me up and steal my candy."

In those days, we didn't even think about having to check the candy for any problems. We ate some of it as we did our trick or treating. But by the time we got home, you wouldn't believe the stacks of candy we had confiscated. The candy bars were only five cents, but they were probably twice as big as the ones today. No one gave out "snack size" candies. They were all the big stuff. Usually we got Hershey Bars, Nestle Bars, Nestle Crunches, Milky Ways, Snickers, Three Musketeers, Baby Ruths, Butterfingers and Tootsie Rolls. One family on Westview Street, the Sweats, even gave out homemade popcorn wrapped in napkins. That was the best house in the neighborhood.

Every once in a while, something would take place which would bring all the kids together, regardless of their ages. Usually we were clearly divided, big kids and little kids. The big kids were three or four years older than the little kids. My brother and all his pals were in the big kids' group. My pals and me were to be known as little kids forever. But when someone would cut a new vine in the woods, little kids were able to hang out with the big kids. A new vine would last maybe a week or two before some grownup figured it was too dangerous and cut it down. But in those few days, it was really quite an event. The best kids would climb high into a tree, have someone swing the vine to him, and go soaring out into the open. Even kids from other neighborhoods might come over in the afternoon or early evening to get in on the fun.

It was about this time that I started to get into music in a pretty big way. One of my favorite TV programs was *The Adventures of Ozzie and Harriet.* The show was pretty good, but my favorite part took place at the end. Rick Nelson would be at the malt shop or dance or something and would sing a song with his guitar and backup band. It seemed like the girls in the audience loved listening to him. I liked that a lot and would often pretend I was Rick Nelson. I started to collect some of his records. I noticed that I could easily sing in his range (still can) and would listen to his albums for hours. My favorite songs were *Teenage Idol, Young World* and *It's Up To You.* I used to close my eyes and wiggle my jaw a little bit, just like he did.

As a matter of fact, the whole family started to get into singing quite a bit that year. *Sing Along With Mitch* was a really popular TV program, and my parents loved it. We would sing songs like *Let Me Call You Sweetheart, Red Red Robin, Keep The Sunnyside Up, Paddlin Maddlin Home, Have You Ever Seen A Dream Walking* and *When Irish Eyes Are Smiling.*

Some of my other favorite TV shows then were *Leave It To Beaver, Andy Griffith, Sheena—Queen of the Jungle* (Boy, she

31

she was hot), and of course, the old reruns of *Superman*. Also, I hate to admit it, but one of my all time favorites, even at the age of nine, was *Mighty Mouse*. He came on every Saturday morning at 10:30, channel 2.

Actually, Saturday mornings were what we lived for all week. As much as I hated to get out of bed Monday through Friday, I had no trouble jumping up early on Saturday mornings. In fact, I would have all my dirty clothes laid out in my room so I wouldn't have to spend much time getting dressed. After playing all morning, sometimes I would tag along with my mother to go to the butcher's shop, known as the Sanzone's Meat Market. The owners were always good to me, slicing off some fresh cheese or bologna and sneaking me some. Mom would let me pick up one of those ten-cent packages of Hostess Cupcakes, Twinkies, or Snowballs, the kind that came in a pack, one white and the other pink, covered in coconut.

From an early age, each kid learned which dogs in the neighborhood were approachable, and which ones were not. Some of our favorites were Bruno, up around the corner, Duke, the Boxer up the street from us, and Willie, the little gray dog that belonged to the Alogna's. However, the little dog next door to us was the Chihuahua from hell. He belonged to the Cove's and, fittingly, his name was Rowdy. Rowdy weighed perhaps fifteen pounds but was by far the most vicious animal known to Hamden. He spent most of the day on a long run in his backyard, which could reach two feet from our property line. When basketballs, footballs or baseballs would occasionally end up in the Cove's yard, you wouldn't even consider going after them. When my brother was just a little boy, he made the mistake of crossing into their yard to pet Rowdy. Rowdy ripped his leg up pretty good. His reputation was set for life. That dog lived longer than any dog I'd ever seen. By the time he was fourteen or fifteen years old, he had lost most of his hair and had a pathetic, hoarse little bark. I don't think he had many teeth left either, but out of respect for a gallant warrior, everyone kept his distance while Rowdy was on patrol.

My real nemesis belonged to the Voulo's, a couple of streets over from us. They had a Boxer named, of all things, Pudgy. Actually, I think Pudgy might have been a pretty friendly dog but for some reason he sensed my fear and would always chase me and jump on me. He never once actually hurt me, but the humiliation factor was enough. Unfortunately, his house was the halfway point between Jimmy Reardon and me, so I had to plot a safe route for getting over to Jimmy's house regularly. I always felt a little bit more in control when I was within running distance of a parked car in somebody's driveway. It was pitiful to see me sprinting towards a car, waiting for a few seconds, venturing out twenty or thirty feet, then running all out again for the next parked car, all the way to Jimmy's house. Pudgy was the bully in my life from ages nine through eleven.

There were other things you learned quickly growing up around Furman Road, too. For instance, you never went near the white house a few doors up from me. The owner was in and out of prison throughout my childhood and we knew enough to stay away from him. I was one of the few people who sort of felt sorry for him and the only one to wave to him and his wife when they drove by. Some of the big kids really took care of his house every Halloween.

We also knew at a very early age which lawns were never to be walked on. The best grass on the street belonged to

Charlie Albanese and his wife, an older couple who had no children. Mr. Albanese would always drive by in a big blue Cadillac, smiling and waving to all the kids, but God help you if a ball went on his lawn and you even thought about getting it back.

We never walked on the lawn across the street from me, either, but it was not out of fear. It was more out of love and respect. This was another older couple named Mr. and Mrs. Pallman who had escaped Germany right before WW II and had settled in Connecticut. Mr. Pallman was a baker, and he and his wife were wonderful to all of us kids. I remember they didn't own a car. They walked everywhere.

When we weren't avoiding dogs and lawns, we spent much of our time in the woods. It was a whole different world: trees to climb, brooks to fall in, a pollywog pond to skate on in the winter, bean fields one, two, and three, and occasionally the setting for a brushfire. Once or twice a year, a kid would get some matches or a magnifying glass and do the deed. The next thing you knew, the word spread up and down the neighborhood, "the woods are on fire." One kid up around the corner had the reputation for being the major arsonist around town. He had a thick pair of eyeglasses and allegedly could start a fire using them like a magnifying glass on a dry leaf.

On the other side of the woods and bean fields, about a half of a mile away, stood a low-income housing project that was actually over the border in New Haven. It didn't mean much to me at the time, but in retrospect, I guess it was rather unusual: the project was completely fenced in, including barbed wire, with only one opening way around on the other side. It was known as Brookside and the inhabitants were the wild and fierce *Brooksiders*. Every once in a while, the word would spread that the "Brooksiders were out!" You never even considered going past Bean Field Number One for several days. Any of the burglaries or vandalism that took place when I was growing up was usually attributed to Brooksiders.

Back at home, my family bought a new hi-fi system to play the Mitch Miller records, and of course, my Rick Nelson albums. We also had an album that I thought was one of the funniest things I had ever heard: The First Family. This was a kind of satire on President Kennedy and all his relatives. I listened to it constantly until I knew each line by heart. I probably learned more about politics from that record than anything else in grammar school. Being huge John Kennedy fans, my family and I just loved it. Also, since I had actually touched the President, I would often stop and watch TV anytime he gave a speech and could imitate him pretty well.

Fads came and went throughout childhood. One of the biggest and best happened in early 1962: Dunkin Yo-yos, Pretty soon everyone had the most popular models: the Butterfly and the Imperial. I could do three things pretty well: walk the dog, go around the world, and rock the cradle. Occasionally, I was accepted for a few minutes into the big kid's circle because I handled a yo-yo as good as any of them. Other fads that came over the next few years included superballs and skateboards. Not many kids actually went out and bought a skateboard. They just took the wheels off of a pair of roller-skates and attached them to a piece of wood.

In the spring of 1962, it was finally time for me to get involved in organized baseball. I was nine years old when

I became a member of a "minor league" team called Chapel Photo. I was given Number Fourteen, certainly not as good as Number Seven or Number Nine, but Bill "Moose" Skowron wasn't a bad name for the Yankees, either. Chapel Photo had kids from age nine through twelve, but any eleven or twelve year old on our team was usually not good enough to make the "majors," which consisted of mostly eleven and twelve year olds and occasionally ten year olds with superstar potential.

I was predominately right handed, but for some reason I was more comfortable batting from the left side. Maybe it was because back then, Yankee Stadium ran 296 feet down the right field line and most of the Yankee greats batted left handed. I had my first official at bat in the first game against the dreaded First Federal team. They were dressed in black and had a pitcher who threw faster than anything I had experienced in practice or in my backyard. I remember clearly how that first pitch came whizzing in there, and me jumping backwards. The umpire hollered, "Strike one!" I regrouped, dug in and waited for the next pitch. Again, another fast ball came blazing in. I jumped out of the way while the umpire bellowed, "Strike two!" My father had always drummed it into our heads that the worst thing in baseball was to look at strike three so I knew I had to swing at the next pitch regardless of where it was, even if it was headed towards my ear. The pitcher went into his windup and threw another hard one. I swung in slow motion and was fortunate enough to catch it right on the meat of the bat, swinging very late. Luckily for me, I lined a clean single right over the third baseman's head into left field. I'll never forget the feeling of standing on that first base bag exchanging my batting helmet for one of those dorky base running helmets, the kind that looked lopsided after two or three strides. I was very proud.

As the season continued, I usually played shortstop and could handle most anything hit near me except I was scared of the hard ground balls that came right at me. I could almost feel the bad hop hitting me square in the nose. As a batter, I don't remember ever striking out, but did not have the same aggressive swing that I had in practice or backyard baseball. My father would constantly talk to me about *pulling* the ball with authority, but regardless of how much I wanted to, I just couldn't seem to make that kind of move in a game. Most of my hits were good, hard, clean singles up the middle. I never did hit one out for a homerun.

A couple of times I was given the chance to pitch a game. My career never went too far there, but one game was a lot of fun. I pitched against Best Cleaners on Sunday afternoon and really had it going. I went the whole game and maybe gave up a couple of hits. I remember wishing the game would not end. I almost didn't want my team to score any runs so we could go a few more extra innings, but we did win handily. A cold Coke after the ball game was one of the sweetest I ever had.

Baseball wasn't our only spring tradition. There was also snake hunting. Down in the swamp that bordered the woods on Jimmy Reardon's side, we would spend a day or two hunting garter snakes and putting them into a big red container. Jimmy, being the expert woodsman, always said the best snake hunting week started on Holy Thursday. Fortunately for us, we always had that afternoon off, and of course, all day Good Friday. We would use a couple of forked sticks to pin the snake down right behind his head, pick it up on the same spot and carry it over to the container. It was especially difficult on a Good Friday afternoon. We were always taught that we shouldn't talk between the hours of 12:00 noon and 3:00 p.m., since that was when Jesus was dying on the cross. We actually would make the effort, snakes and all, but I think our record may have lasted four minutes.

Besides baseball and snakes, one of the best things about fourth grade happened on Thursday nights: dancing lessons. Howie and I had to go to Williams Ballroom, Hamden, Connecticut, every Thursday night during the school year from 7:00 p.m. to 8:00 p.m. There were three adults who did the instructing: Mr. Williams, Mrs. Williams and their assistant, Mr. Anderson. They would watch us closely as we practiced our waltz or cha-cha.

All our parents sat off to the side, whispering to each other and nodding their approval while we kept up with our one-two-three, one-two-three. For many of the nine to thirteen year olds, Thursdays in '61–'62 were something they had simply learned to accept. I was different. They were my favorite and most important nights of the week.

Preparations began at 6:00 p.m. at home with Boraxo soap to clean the hands thoroughly, a selection of jacket and tie, and the crowning touch: a quart of Vitalis in the hair. I was nine, my brother thirteen, and I thought I was pretty cool. I had as much confidence on that ballroom floor every week as any of the *big kids* in the class.

Good manners were critical. Before the cha-cha began, or fox trot, or rumba, the young gentleman would approach the young lady with the question, "May I please have this dance?" Then you would begin, right hand holding the middle of her back, right elbow sticking out high for her to rest her arm if it grew tired, and feet moving to the music with the steps you practiced over and over.

Not to sound cocky, but I knew I was one of the better dancers. I had been promoted to the class of the older kids during the year, and certainly enjoyed the attention of being the youngest. But more importantly, I could also be nearer to who I felt was perhaps the most beautiful woman that God ever created: Betty Jane Maturo, fifth grader, big brown eyes, long wavy brown hair. A young Sophia Loren.

It wasn't just me, either. She turned everyone's head. Betty Jane had the style and grace of, well, a seventh or eighth grader. I knew my brother and his friends admired her, too.

Being a year younger and fully understanding the difference in our social status, I was content to dance with just about everyone else that spring. Oh, I could gaze from a distance, even catch a whiff of that wonderful scent when she floated by, but it never occurred to me to ask her to dance. I knew my place.

In April, my admiration for her beauty and style suddenly moved up several notches to hopeless but intense love. This was the night Mr. and Mrs. Williams had called for a "Shipwreck Party." We were all to dress accordingly. Mom hauled out t-shirts and old jeans with some strips cut in them and said we were ready. I think I found a straw hat, too.

The other kids were similarly decked out, some more "shipwrecked" than others. There was, however, one exception. Betty Jane made a fashionably late entrance as the "Island Princess" of wherever we were supposed to be shipwrecked. She was only covered, so it seemed, in green leaves and flowers. I never saw anything like it. The Vitalis started evaporating. I was a dead man.

A waltz ended, and as was the custom, it was time for "ladies choice," a cruel turn of events where the gentlemen stayed on the floor and the ladies came out to do the asking. A fox trot began and the running and giggles followed. Through these moments of chaos and all around embarrassment, I detected a blur of green leaves heading in my direction, lost it for a second and then picked it up again. I assumed Betty Jane was moving across the floor to ask one of the coolest kids for a dance. At least I would be able to catch a whiff of that great perfume she wore. I was hoping she'd ask someone near me.

Oh no, Oh no. She was looking at me. Eye contact. Oh no, she smiled . . . Oh no, "May I please have this dance?" A mumbled yes from me and she was in my arms: leaves, flowers, brown hair and that wonderful smell. I was shaking so badly I could hardly dance.

Betty Jane may have actually tried to have a conversation with me, but I was incapable. I was simply mumbling to myself over and over, "Please don't wake up. Please don't wake up."

Somewhere I had seen something about our President and Mrs. Kennedy living in a place known as "Camelot." Maybe they did, but they weren't alone. For one nine-year-old boy at Williams Ballroom Studio in Hamden, Connecticut, for one brief shining moment . . .

Spring 1962 was remarkable in more ways than one. It might have been the biggest year for baseball cards. We were coming off the sixty-one homeruns belted by Roger Maris the year before and a New York Yankees' World Series win over the Cincinnati Reds, and my friends and I were playing organized baseball for the first time. There was nothing like going up to Al's Superette on our bikes to buy a pack of baseball cards for a nickel. These were Topp's cards, and they came in a yellow wrapper with a big stick of pink bubblegum. The cards smelled great, just like bubblegum, for a couple of weeks. It was wonderful buying a pack, going behind the store and slowly unwrapping it to see who you got. Every year the most important two cards were Mickey Mantle and the New York Yankees' team picture. I never liked when those cards came out in the first series. It meant there was a little bit of a letdown with the other series of cards.

Every once in a while back at Saint John's recess, one of the older kids would decide to start a riot using his baseball cards. Out of the clear blue, someone would fire up one card after another into the air. You should have seen every boy in that schoolyard fight wildly, stomping the ground, diving into piles to get that free card. Sometimes, the nuns would try to stop it, because it was really bedlam and at that point, the instigator would usually take his remaining fifty or one hundred cards and throw them all up at the same time, scattering in all directions. I never saw anything like it in my life.

Howie was preparing to graduate from the eighth grade that spring. There was an eighth grade picnic at Lake Quasapaug, an amusement park about an hour from our school. My mother was one of the chaperones, so Maureen and I got to tag along. I spent the day hanging out with some of the eighth graders and had an absolute ball. It must have had a big effect on me, because for a long time, I had many dreams about that amusement park.

One of the most exciting times of every year was the week before school let out. The nuns were always in good moods, every recess seemed to be a little longer, and the bus ride every afternoon back home was completely different than the norm. We would usually start singing. One of my favorite lyrics was "Five more days and we'll be free, honey . . . five more days and we'll be free, babe . . . five more days and we'll be free, from this penitentiary, honey oh baby my." We also got to wear casual clothes on the last couple days of school. Usually, we had to wear a navy blue blazer, gray pants, white shirt and tie. The very last day of school was a half-day session, and the anticipation of getting out at noon was fantastic.

Besides the usual whiffle ball games and fort building, one of our summer traditions was waiting for the ice cream men. Occasionally, we would see the Good Humor guy, but the man who had the entire market share of our neighborhood was *Joe* who drove the Ding Dong truck. Besides great ice cream bars for a dime, Joe would hand out things like caps and water pistols. He was a great fellow who knew every kid's name. He handled the Furman Road area for years.

That summer, I cheated on Joe a couple of times. *Mister Softee* started hitting our neighborhood and I tried it out. This was soft ice cream and was pretty good. Unfortunately, he came about an hour before Joe did, so I would hide in the house or down the woods when I heard the Ding Dong truck rolling through. I simply couldn't face Joe after what I had done.

Summer nights were as good as summer days. When darkness began to fall, the big kids would allow the little kids to play in the same big game they were organizing. Most often it was a gigantic game of hide and go seek. Sometimes, there would be twenty of us running all over the neighborhood laughing and carrying on. I always noticed that when I found the perfect hiding spot, I had to go the bathroom. I guess you never noticed it when you were running around, but as soon as you stayed still, you started wiggling all over. Usually, I had to run down the woods or go home before I burst.

The other games that were popular were freeze tag, spud, one two three red light and television tag, one of my favorites. Right before whoever was *It* was about to tag you, you would fall down and yell out the name of a TV program. You could never call out a name that was already used that night. This was an area where I shone.

Summer was also a great time for simply curb sitting with some of my pals. There were some pretty good philosophical discussions just sitting in the shade of a tree by the hour. Even at that age we would sometimes get into talks about religion and church. I always found it fascinating to hear from all my Jewish friends, who were taught that they were still waiting for the Messiah. I was a little confused about what I had learned in my religion, especially when the nuns were teaching. According to them, the Jewish people and Protestants would not go to Hell since "it wasn't their fault," but they would not have the same place in heaven as we Catholics.

I wasn't sure if I believed this completely, but I didn't want to take any chances with Bonnie Lipton, my best girl who happened to be Jewish. She was the girl I expected to marry someday, and I didn't want to go through life with the outside chance that Bonnie would not be in the same place in heaven with me a hundred years from now. So, one afternoon, I took the garden hose and baptized her. It was supposed to be our secret, but Bonnie would give it away now and then when she would reach down into the water of a swimming pool with her right hand, touch it, and proceed to bless herself before swimming.

I always hated it when summer began to wind down. We savored those last couple of weeks more than any other time.

Chapter Six

1962–1963

Atomic Bombs and Jackie Gleason

I began the fifth grade at Saint John's in September. My teacher was Mother St. Maureen, a wonderful nun with flaming red hair, at least the tiny bit we could see. My favorite subjects were American History and Geography. I taught myself how to name each president of the United States, going all the way up to President Kennedy. I could also name the state capitals of all 50 states.

A few big things happened that October. First of all, the Yankees were in a terrific seven game World Series against the San Francisco Giants. We got home just in time to listen to the ball games on the radio after school. I remember Willie McCovey of the Giants smashing a line drive out toward the right side of the field that could have won the game, but fortunately it was directed at second baseman

Bobby Richardson, who held on to the World Series with the catch. The Yanks would get to the Series in '63 and '64, but would not win again until Reggie Jackson's three homeruns in the sixth game took the Series from the Dodgers in 1977.

I also became a big New York Giants fan. Whatever we played, touch football in the street or tackle on the side of my yard, we always pretended we were Y. A. Tittle, Aaron Thomas or Frank Gifford. Grandma Murphy finally had an old black and white TV set at her house so I was able to catch the Giants games with one of my great aunts, Ann Butler, who was probably in her late seventies.

My birthday was coming up on October 23rd, and in keeping with the Murphy family tradition, I was allowed to have my first "kids only" birthday party. We could only have one at the age of five and the age of ten. The rest of the parties were relatives and grownups.

A few days before my birthday, most of the attention from my parents and the nuns at school centered on something that was happening in Cuba. Feeling that I had a sort of personal connection to President Kennedy, I was very much aware of what was going on. I watched all the newscasts and even read the newspapers. It was the "Missiles of October" crisis, and I was concerned my upcoming birthday party was never going to be.

I distinctly remember doing a lot of praying at school, led by our nuns, and it was very frightening to me. I knew all about atomic bombs and I really felt there was the distinct possibility that each day I went to school might be my last. I had seen a number of those bomb shelters on display at the neighborhood shopping center and suddenly wished the Murphy family had one. My friends disappointed me a little bit because they really didn't have a clue as to what was going on. I thought I was the only one in my age group who was really scared. I was afraid of being burned up, and President Kennedy looked pretty grim.

October 23rd did come, and I remember blowing out the candles on my cake after making my wish. Instead of the usual wish for the New York Giants next game being a victory or a certain girl in my class noticing me, I said a quick prayer that there would not be an atomic war. I always felt partially responsible for that crisis ending peacefully.

That fall I fell in love again, heavily. This time, too, it was an older woman. A new show, *The Beverly Hillbillies*, made its debut on CBS, and it was love at first sight for Elly May Clampett, played by Donna Douglas. Over the years, she would be replaced with the likes of Barbara Eden of *I Dream of Genie*, Elizabeth Montgomery of *Bewitched* and Tina Louise of *Gilligan's Island*. Unfortunately, we had very strict bed times in the Murphy house and I was supposed to be in bed just at the time *Beverly Hillbillies* was starting. I would sneak down the stairs to catch a glimpse of her until I was caught and sent back up to bed. Howie, always the sensitive soul, would make things worse by explaining to me in great detail the next day how Elly May was in a bathing suit, lounging around the "cement pond." It must have been the forbidden fruit theory, because by the next year, I was able to stay up late enough to see her and, surprisingly, I was not all that jealous when she began falling for a guy named "Dash Riprock."

Television was big in our home. You knew exactly what day it was and what time it was by what was on television. When we got back from Ansonia on Saturday night, one of the more fun traditions was the whole family sitting down to watch *The Jackie Gleason Show*. My parents would really howl during this program, but we all lived for the last few minutes of the show. That's when Frank Fontaine did the Crazy Gugheheine act. We thought he was an absolute riot. Then at the end of the skit, Joe the Bartender would tell some unseen patron to "drop a nickel into number seven," and Crazy would sing a song, very serious and very well.

One of the highlights of the year (lowlights in my parents' eyes) was when Mom and Dad had a bunch of people over from Dad's office. Some pretty important people had their winter coats and hats upstairs, lying on the bed. Howie dared me to put on one of the coats, pull down one of the hats over my ears and go downstairs as Crazy Gugheheine. When I walked into the cocktail party and began my routine I thought my father was going to kill me but, thank God, I got enough laughs from the guests to save myself from certain death.

Another great tradition in the '60s was the annual showing of *The Wizard of Oz.* Of course, nowadays you can rent the video any time you want, but half of the fun of that movie was the anticipation of the event. It was normally shown on Sunday night, and the whole family was parked in front of the television getting ready for it. The best character by far was the Cowardly Lion. My favorite scenes were with the flying monkeys and the soldiers who marched into the witch's castle. I lived for the moment when the Scarecrow, the Tin Man and the Cowardly Lion dressed up as those soldiers and marched into the castle with them, the Lion desperately trying to keep his tail under the long coat. I even had a lump in my throat each year when Dorothy said good-bye to the Scarecrow.

On Friday nights, my family tore itself away from the television to do our grocery shopping. For years, we all went together, but as we kids grew older, Mom and Dad let Howie and me stay at home. As soon as they left, we would start all kinds of experiments involving the creation of a super chocolate ice cream soda. Then we would move the furniture and practice our professional wrestling techniques. I was usually the character named "Argentina Apollo." Howie always like to be the World Wresting Champion, Bruno Samartino.

When my parents and Maureen returned, Howie and I would go out to help bring in bags of groceries. Once in a while, there would be a searchlight from one of the car dealerships a mile away. There was nothing like a bitter cold Friday night, Howie and I racing across the yard and trying to beat the searchlight in the night sky full of stars.

Once in a while, Dad would spot the Telstar Satellite and try to show us. On many occasions, we were able to see it moving right across the sky. He was always pretty good about showing the neighborhood kids, too, if they happened to be around.

Weekends were always something so special to me. I would often come home from school and make sure I got all my homework done that afternoon so I had nothing hanging over my head the rest of the weekend. We had a rule in my house: if your homework was not completed by Sunday morning, you could not go outside or watch television after church until you had done it all. Funny enough, I either did it on Friday afternoon or Sunday mornings after church. I don't remember ever doing it Friday night or Saturday.

Another thing I liked about Friday nights were the frozen squares of pizza my mother would heat up as snacks. This was something new to our Irish family. Up until that time, the only Italian food allowed in our house were cans of Franco American spaghetti or Chef Boy R Dee spaghetti which we kids might have for a Saturday lunch. My father had to have meat and potatoes just about every night.

The Flintstones was a big Friday night show then, and usually the squares of pizza would come out just as the program was beginning. Even to a ten year old like me, you could see the similarity between that show and the old *Honeymooners.* It was pretty clever.

That winter, my father began a big project. He was going to finish off the basement, and Howie and I were going to help. Usually, we hated anything to do with helping my father do a job, but finishing off the basement turned out to be a lot of fun. Watching the cellar slowly turn from a bunch of concrete walls and a furnace into beautiful planks of pinewood and tiles was remarkable.

The basement turned out to be a perfect place for me whenever I wanted a little privacy. We eventually had a couple of chairs and a couch down there, a black and white television, built-in toy boxes and an electric heater for the winter.

Dad also got us a ping-pong table which I practiced on for hours each week, hitting the ball into the wall and bouncing it back on the table. I became petty good at the game, and could compete with my father and my brother. Unfortunately, as I approached the magic number of twenty-one points against Howie, I had to keep my mind not only on the game, but also on the more than likely chance a ping-pong paddle would come flying at my head if I even had the slightest victorious smile on my face. A good sport he was not when it came to losing to his little brother. Any time I played Howie in ping-pong, I made sure I was closest to the stairs in case I needed to make a fast exit.

I practically lived in that finished-off basement. One week, I fell in love yet again, this time with an Italian actress who was on the *Million Dollar Movie* on Channel 9 out of New York City. The same movie would be on every week night. The opening theme to the *Million Dollar Movie* was the same music from *Gone With the Wind.* Anyway, I was fiddling with the channels when I came across a bunch of Roman Legions doing the usual thing, fighting against the "Barbarians." The movie was called *The Slave of Rome.*

The leader of the Barbarians was an absolute goddess who had a helmet with horns on it. She fought with a sword and shield almost as good as any of her men. After one good fight, she was captured by the Roman general who naturally fell in love with her. They decided they wanted to live in peace with the Barbarians, but the new leader who replaced her was really evil and did not like the fact that the woman had gone over to the other side.

There was going to be one big battle, but my clearest memory is not of the fighting, but the sound of the trumpets when the Roman soldiers were marching toward the valley where the Barbarians awaited. That music has stayed in my head for decades. It was haunting.

Too bad, I was only able to watch *The Slave of Rome* for those five days. I never saw the movie again and to this day, I still check *TV Guide* every week to see if the movie might be there. I even called someone at Channel 9 a couple of years ago to see if the station might have it in its archives. It didn't. Maybe the movie is under another name. I don't know, but I would give anything to see it again.

It was about this time that I was old enough to go to the Strand Theater, which was about a half a mile from my home. Every once in a while when we didn't have to go out to the Valley to see our grandmothers, I might go up to the

Strand to see a movie with Jimmy Reardon. Still not fully recovered from *The Slave of Rome,* anything that had Roman soldiers or even Greek soldiers had to be seen. Some of my favorites were *The Fall of Rome, Hercules, Hercules Unchained,* and *Jason and the Golden Fleece.* It was thirty-five cents to get in if you were under twelve, fifty cents for the older kids. Mom would give me an extra ten cents to spend on candy. I either bought two bars of candy for a nickel each or one box of popcorn for a dime. A couple of years later there was a penny tax on the ten cents, so Mom had to give me eleven cents.

The biggest problem with being so fascinated with Roman Legions (helmets, swords and shields) was when I played *war* with my friends. I spent a lot of time at my father's workbench building wooden swords and a shield. My weapons and armor could not hold up against the plastic machine guns the other kids had. I was always the first one who was killed, even though I clearly looked the coolest.

In the spring of 1963, it was time for Easter. Even though I hated when Lent was over, I did enjoy the Easter Egg Hunt my father organized out in the yard. One of my least proud moments came that spring when Bonnie came over and Dad invited her to join in the fun.

It was one of those situations where you know you are acting like a complete jerk, but you still can't stop yourself. You knew you were completely wrong, but continued down the path of terrible behavior. I kept complaining to my father and anyone else within earshot that it was not fair for Bonnie to be getting so many eggs, especially since she was Jewish! I really had the right Christian spirit. I think I was finally sent into the house after three or four warnings. As I said, it was not one of my finer moments.

Easter Sunday usually had some of the same excitement as Christmas. There was a little bit of anticipation of the treats we were going to get when we woke up that morning but on a much smaller scale. Three Easter baskets were hidden around the house that Howie, Maureen and I had to find. There was always a big chocolate bunny in the middle of the basket surrounded by jelly beans and yellow chicks. Maureen and I always had the regular chocolate, but Howie had to have white chocolate. Sometimes the normal milk chocolate would bring on an asthma attack. Some of the kids in the neighborhood would get bigger chocolate bunnies, but they were usually hollow. We always got the solid ones.

In May of each year, St. John's had a big deal called the "May Crowning." This was some sort of celebration for the Blessed Virgin Mary. An eighth-grade girl would get all dressed up and march into the church, go up a ladder to the statue of Mary and place a crown of flowers on her head. It didn't have the excitement and flavor of say, a Midnight Mass, but it was always a good looking girl who got to be the May Queen. She was usually pretty famous for a few weeks.

That spring I was "called up" from the Minors to the Majors in baseball. That was a pretty big honor for a ten year old. I usually got to play half the game and that was in the outfield but I thought I was pretty cool wearing the full uniform. Minor Leaguers only had a cap and shirt, but the Major Leaguers had everything, including the pants and stirrup socks. We also got to play at Pine Rock Field, which attracted the most fans.

We usually had a game once or twice between Monday and Friday, starting at 6:00 p.m. What I really liked was an early Saturday game, especially if we won and I played well. Then I would not go home with my family but would hang around the field for the next two or three games, proudly strutting about in my Hamden Plaza uniform. I was now wearing Number 10, Tony Kubec of the Yankees. Not bad.

As May turned into June, Connecticut burst out in honeysuckles. I would go picking them many nights with Billy, Bonnie, and another friend up the street, Debbie Heinz. We would pull the honeysuckle stem down through the bottom very slowly until it made a little bubble and we would suck the juice out. Nothing tasted or smelled better than honeysuckles in the late spring. One time we picked hundreds and saved them in my garage for a week, but that didn't work out at all.

School was winding down again, and it was time for our final report cards. In the third quarter, I had received my best grades ever: thirteen As and four Bs. In the fourth quarter, I "slipped" to twelve As and five Bs. It actually bothered me.

I think that was the summer that Billy Meinson, a kid who lived a street over from me on Westview, was hit by a car right on the street next to my house, Thomas. It must have been a weekend, because my father was out trimming the hedges and was the first one to get to Billy. He was a year younger than me, not one of my closest friends, but we often played together in big crowds. I did not see the crash but sure did hear it and went tearing over to see what had happened.

Apparently Billy was on a bike and came right out of Westview into the path of a car coming down Thomas Street. He was covered in blood and was somehow trying to get up on his feet and run home when my father caught him and laid him down on the side of the road. The car that hit him had a shattered windshield where Billy's head had smashed, and his hair and blood were all over the glass. I never saw so much blood in my life. Billy was quite conscious and yelling out, "Am I going to die?" I'll bet a hundred people were there in a matter of minutes. My father told me to run into the house and get my pillow and plenty of towels.

It's funny what you remember when things like that happen. When I came flying out of the house with the pillow and towels, right there between the crowd and me was my old nemesis, Pudgy the dog. He barely looked at me as I went running past him on the way to Billy and my father. An ambulance showed up a few minutes later, and the medics took over. The police were there for a long time asking if anyone had seen it actually happen, but I don't think anyone did. You could still smell the blood even hours later, and the stains were there until the next rain. Billy would recover, and a few days later, his father stopped by my house to shake hands with my father, thanking him for all his help.

Soon after that we were off to Cape Cod again for another two weeks of Kennedy watching. We did not know it, of course, but it was to be the last time for that.

Chapter Seven

1963–1964

Oswald and The Beatles

ack at Saint John the Baptist for the sixth grade, my new teacher was Mother St. Michael Raymond, pretty young but with a reputation for being very strict. She had been Howie's teacher four years earlier. Maureen was also starting first grade at St. John's. She and I had to wait for the school bus each morning out in front of our house.

We settled into the school year and the Yanks were blown out in the World Series, four straight against the Los Angeles Dodgers. Meanwhile, Jimmy Reardon and I set a new personal record for numbers of candy bars collected on Halloween.

One Friday afternoon in November, my sixth grade class was busy doing artwork, which I did not like very much. All the other kids in class looked forward to Friday afternoon art, but I struggled in that area. I was always the one who was two or three steps behind the rest of the class. My scissors cutting and gluing skills were pathetic. Everything I made was lopsided and sloppy.

That afternoon, the voice of Mother Superior came over the PA system. She announced to the entire school that President Kennedy had been wounded by gunfire in Dallas, Texas, while riding in a car. We were all to stop our work and begin praying. Mother St. Michael looked terrible and was in and out of the classroom for the next half hour or so. Lots of nuns and lay teachers were hanging around the hallways.

Unfortunately, it was time for another one of my insensitive episodes. I remember clearly how we were all marched to the bathrooms for our afternoon visit. I was standing at one of the urinals, Jimmy Reardon on my right, and I was whispering to him "You know, if he dies, we get Monday off." Later on, back in class, Mother St. Michael left the room again and the class was getting restless and making a lot of noise. A few minutes later, the other sixth grade teacher, Mother St. Joseph, burst into our class and started yelling at all of us to quiet down and behave. She hollered out, "How can you act like this, with your president dead?" A couple of girls asked her if it was true. All we had heard was that he was wounded. Mother explained to us that it was just announced that he had been declared dead a few minutes earlier.

That afternoon when I got off the bus, there were lots of mothers standing around talking about it. *The New Haven Register,* the late afternoon edition, had the biggest headline I had ever seen, two and a half inches with the words "KENNEDY SLAIN!" Right underneath it was smaller print about a half inch in size, "Texas Governor

Also Wounded In Shooting." I read that newspaper from cover to cover and sat in front of the television by the hour, taking it all in. My parents let me stay up late that night, and I did not miss a thing. I saw things that had a big impression on me.

I don't remember the new president giving much of a speech, but I know he tried. I do remember the sight of Mrs. Kennedy vividly, bloodstains on her dress, her not being able to open the door of an ambulance. I also remember the arms reaching up to her to help her down out of Air Force 1, the same jet I had seen over and over again up on Cape Cod. The look on Bobby Kennedy's face told me that my favorite comedy record *The First Family* was not going to be heard much anymore in our house. Camelot was over.

The next day, I again read the paper from cover to cover. I was engrossed in all the details of the shooting, where the first bullet hit and how it went through the back of his neck and out his throat. They said the next one blew off the top of his head.

I had that same kind of feeling I had a year earlier and wondered if this might be the beginning of something that would lead to an atomic war. I remember the newscasters reading a statement from Chairman Khruschev in the Soviet Union. There were very nice words for the American people and especially for Mrs. Kennedy and her children. I felt a lot better about the chances of not having a nuclear war, at least that day.

All weekend it was the same story over and over again. The television camera was on that flag-draped casket for hours. On Sunday, just before we sat down to eat, it was announced that Lee Harvey Oswald was going to be moved through the police garage. I was not in the room where the TV was, but someone in my family started yelling out that

Oswald had been shot. We all ran to get in front of the television set as they showed replay after replay of Jack Ruby sticking a gun into Oswald's stomach and firing. Even at the age of eleven, I could not believe how stupid it was to allow anyone with a gun in that area. I figured we would never know why John Kennedy was murdered.

That afternoon, I was over at Jimmy Reardon's street and there were a lot of kids hanging around talking about all the events. I felt pretty important because I seemed to know a lot more about everything. Most of them didn't know about the policeman, Officer Tibbit, who was also part of the story.

Just as I predicted, we had Monday off. However, it was not such a fun day. I spent most of it over at Jimmy's house down in his basement with him and his father, watching the funeral procession. It was the first time I had ever seen flags at something called "half mast." I was fascinated by the riderless horse and the boots turned backwards in the stirrups. It really hit me when Kennedy's son, John Jr., stepped out and snapped a salute to his father as the wagon rolled slowly by carrying the body. It was a long day.

It's strange how life goes on, even after that terrible weekend, because that same month, my family was in the market for a new car. Up to that point, our main car was a 1954 blue and white Chevy. A couple of years earlier, we had picked up an even older car from Uncle Phil, a jet black Plymouth. Now it was time to get rid of that car and look for a new one. We finally settled on a dark greenish-blue Chevrolet Impala, the 1964 model. This was our first car with a radio. The thing I remember the most, however, was the wonderful smell that seemed to linger for months. It was also a lot of fun having just about every neighbor stop over in our driveway to take a good look at it and shake hands with my father, wishing him luck.

That winter, Jimmy and I got fifty cents each and bought a small green turtle at the pet store for a dollar. The plan was for me keep it for one week then bring it over to Jimmy's house on Saturday, where he would keep it for the next week. We named him Poochie. If Friday nights were a great time for me growing up, then those Friday nights before Poochie's visit were even better. Jimmy and I spent a lot of time looking after that turtle.

One evening a couple of days before I was to get Poochie back at my house, the phone rang and it was Jimmy. He sounded pretty solemn. He told me that he had bad news . . . Poochie was dead. I could barely choke out the words, "How did it happen?" Jimmy replied, "A mouse ate him." That's when I lost it. Jimmy went on to explain that there was nothing left but his shell. It turned out that there was not even enough left of him for a good burial.

Although spring and summer were my favorite seasons, winter also had some benefits. Snowball fights, snowforts and sled riding were times of great fun. There was a small hill right behind Jimmy's house where we took our sleds on most winter afternoons. He and I became pretty proficient at standing up on our sleds and driving them with the ropes, dueling in a sort of chariot race together.

However, the real excitement was the anticipation of the occasional "snow day." There was nothing like going to bed on a Tuesday night with a big snowstorm starting outside. You would just lie there hoping against hope that there would be at least a foot of snow and you would not have school for a day or two. Several times throughout the night, I would look outside and be amazed by how bright it was with the white snow covering everything. It was hard to believe it was midnight when you could see so much around the neighborhood.

When it was time to get up in the morning, we would all be huddled around the radio, listening to WELI, holding our breaths for the school cancellations. When it was finally announced that St. John the Baptist was closed, the thrill was unimaginable. The phone would immediately ring, and Jimmy Reardon and I would make our plans for the day.

If it was too cold, the snow was not right for making snowballs or snow forts, so it usually meant a day of sled riding. Sometimes we would go over to Pine Rock Field, where there was a tremendous hill. We would go so fast on the hill that we couldn't even consider showing off our chariot racing skills.

One Saturday during that winter, I must have been a little bored, so I did what was part of my job description for an eleven year old: torment my younger sister. She had a Barbie doll with a miniature kitchen set. It included a refrigerator, stove, pots and pans and three tiny white eggs. I started taking a few of the things away from her until she began to cry. To really frustrate her, I took one of the eggs and hid it in my ear, allowing her to check all over me, to prove that I really didn't have it. When Maureen got upset enough, Mom started yelling at me to stop teasing her, so it was time to give back the little egg.

Unfortunately, I couldn't quite get it out. After about ten minutes of trying, it was time to go out and face my parents. After a couple of minutes of scolding, Dad got a flashlight and a pair of tweezers and began working on my ear. He started saying that he could not get it out . . . he was making it worse by pushing it in even further. He could not believe how ridiculous this was and ultimately had to face the prospect of taking me to the emergency room for such a thing. I wasn't very happy, either, because I knew I was going to look like an idiot. This was not going to be a case of looking *macho* after a trip to the hospital. It was not like I had broken a leg playing football. Also, my Saturday was being cut into.

When we arrived at Saint Raphael's Hospital, we were told to stay in the waiting room. *Real* emergencies were coming in all morning, broken arms, heart attacks, bad cuts with lots of blood, etc. When a nurse came by with a clipboard and asked my father what the trouble was, he just shrugged and nodded his head toward me. I sat with my head cocked to one side, so the egg would not go in any further, looked up at her, and said that I had an egg in my ear. She just stood there with her mouth open looking at me.

We finally got in to see one of the doctors, and he began to poke into my ear with a long pair of tweezers but he did not have any more luck than Dad. He thought it was getting too close to the eardrum. There was one thing he could try, and if that didn't work, they might have to perform minor surgery. I could not believe the trouble I had gotten into this time. Anyway, he filled my ear up with some slippery oil and used a long black rubber tube that was attached to a sort of vacuum. In a matter of seconds, it came out. We were home fifteen minutes later. It made sense to me that every household should have one of those rubber tubes to get things out of ears, and I mentioned this to my father. He did not answer me.

In January 1964, I noticed that a girl in my class, Susan Wall, had a bunch of buttons stuck on everything, from her book bag to her notebooks. They reminded me of the kind of campaign buttons I had seen when John Kennedy was running for president in 1960. But these buttons simply said the same thing, "The Beatles are Coming!!" I didn't have a clue as to what that meant. A few days later, I heard the same expression on a newscast. Again, I had no idea what it was all about. I finally asked my father what it meant and he shook his head and explained to me that it was about some guys from England who sang songs and had long hair. He said they all looked like Moe from the Three Stooges.

A few weeks later, everyone at school and the radio announcers were talking about how "The Beatles" were going to be on *The Ed Sullivan Show* the following Sunday night. The Murphy family watched that program every week, so I knew I was finally going to see what all the fuss was about. I was also hearing *I Want to Hold Your Hand* and *She Loves You* every time the radio was on, but nothing prepared me for the spectacle and excitement coming that February night. At 8:00 p.m., we were all parked in front of the TV.

I think what got to me more than anything else was the audience. The girls were screaming at the top of their lungs, and some appeared to be ready to faint from the hysteria. Meanwhile, the four Beatles seemed to be enjoying all the commotion, just smiling and belting out their songs.

I became an instant fan. I studied each of their movements carefully, like Paul playing with his feet together and moving his head from side to side. He seemed to get the loudest screams when the camera was on him and he smiled the most. Ringo also appeared to be very happy with the frenzy, just pounding away on his drums but not singing. He kept bobbing his head to the side, and his hair shook. George seemed to be the solemn one, but I liked the way he would move over to Paul's microphone and sing back-up harmony with him. The girls really went crazy when the two of them would lean into the mike. By far, however, my favorite was John. I loved the way he had his feet spread apart, almost like a shortstop getting ready to take on a ground ball. Instead of moving his head back and forth sideways like Paul, he sort of kept it right on the microphone, constantly sizing up the audience and occasionally revealing a sly grin. He looked like he expected the madness and was clearly in charge.

Needless to say, I was finished with Rick Nelson. I paid seventy nine cents and got my first Beatles 45 record, *I Want to Hold Your Hand* on one side and *I Saw Her Standing There* on the other. I listened to those two songs for hours and stared at the little jacket the record came in, the one with the picture of them posed around a chair, Paul McCartney holding a cigarette. In the evenings when I was supposed to be doing my homework, 5:30 p.m. to 7:30 p.m., I would play my brother's little brown transistor radio, which came with an ear plug. The song I looked most forward to each night was *P.S. I Love You*. Once 7:30 p.m. came, I would go out in the kitchen and eat bowls of cereal, listening to the big radio. The New Haven radio station, WAVZ, Lucky 13 on the dial, was more or less the official Beatles station. I would stay out there all evening until it was time to go to bed. Then I would again listen to the transistor radio, falling asleep with that ear plug hanging off me.

A few weeks later, I bought my second Beatles record, this time four songs on the 45. Jimmy Reardon was lucky enough to have the album *Meet The Beatles* at his house. I think it belonged to his older sister, Joyce. We would listen to it every afternoon down in his basement. The songs were all great, but I needed to hear the one called *You Can't Do That*. Once on *The Ed Sullivan Show*, there was a video tape of the band playing that song somewhere in Europe and the heart-pounding beat had the girls on fire.

I didn't get my hands on that song until I finally got my own album, *The Beatles Second Album.*

My grades started to slip, but I just couldn't stay away from their music. I used to become very impatient with any of my friends who could not figure out who the lead singer was for every one of their songs. To me it was easy to distinguish the different sounds of McCartney's voice and Lennon's.

I remember grabbing an old tennis racket and pretending it was a guitar while I sang along with the records. I made my little sister sit in front of me on the couch and applaud and scream while I went through my *sets,* even down to the formal bow at the end of each number. I was pretty good on that tennis racket.

That spring, Beatle cards were taking the place of baseball cards at St. John's. I would look at them for hours while I played their music over and over. One of my favorite cards was the one with some trick photography showing the four Beatles with crew cuts.

We had a new girl at school, and it was generally felt by the boys that she was the prettiest girl in our class. She was blonde with great big eyes. Her name was Carol Brennan. She quickly rose in the social ranks at St. John's and hung around the other good looking girls and the toughest guys. She really didn't have much to do with my friends and me but every once in a while, she would be quietly singing a Beatles tune while we were over by the lockers, getting our jackets on to go out to recess. Perhaps, she knew that I was an authority on The Beatles. One day she drummed on my back softly while she hummed one of their songs. That day, I walked a little taller.

There were other changes in my life at that time, too. Most of the "cool" kids had a girlfriend by now, and I thought it was time for me to have one as well. Naturally, I turned to the only woman in my life, Bonnie Lipton, across the street. She agreed to be my official girlfriend, so that was the case for the rest of the sixth grade. Actually, I never went anywhere with her, we never held hands, and things were basically the same as always. However, I could tell people that I had a girlfriend.

Jimmy Reardon and I were starting to hit the social circles, too. Father Kevin would occasionally put together a roller skating trip to a rink in Middletown, about forty five minutes away from school. On Friday nights, we would climb in a bus and head out. At the rink, you would summon up enough courage to ask a girl to skate with you. This was a chance to hold a girl's hand and try to look as cool as you possibly could. I could never figure out why the best looking girls at St. John's always seemed to hang around with guys who were always getting into trouble. On the bus ride from skating, they would usually be in the back of the bus "making out." There was a lot of cigarette smoking on the bus, too.

Once in a while, I would sleep over at Jimmy's house, especially on Saturdays after a day of ice skating at Edgewood Park in New Haven. His parents would take us out to eat, and thanks to them, I experienced real Italian pizza for the first time in my life. It was wonderful. Mr. Reardon teased me about how much pizza I could eat and always kidded me about putting the next meal "on the bill" as well as the night's accommodations. The Reardon's were like a second family.

That same year, Mother St. Michael announced the names of six or seven boys who were to please stand up and go to Mothers Superior's office. I couldn't figure out what I had done, but felt a little better when I saw a few of the boys from the other sixth grade waiting there, too. They were all good kids and the best students. I figured that I wasn't in any trouble. A few minutes later, Father Frisbee came in and explained to us that we had been recommended by the nuns to be the newest altar boys of St. John's. This was quite an honor. All of us were thrilled, and Father Frisbee told us that training would start the following Monday. We were all to get out of class an hour early every other day for a couple of weeks while we learned how to serve Mass and memorize Latin.

The Latin part wasn't difficult, since I had been hearing it every Sunday morning for years. But there was a lot of stuff we had to practice like how to hold our hands in prayer, how to wash the priest's hands, and how to ring the bell at the right times.

The big day finally arrived with me serving Mass on a weekday morning at 7:30 a.m. You were not allowed to take a Sunday Mass until you had proven yourself during the week. Sunday was Prime Time. My family came to my first Mass, and I was on the *Book* side as opposed to the *Bells* side. The altar boy who was on the left was responsible for moving the large book from one side of the altar to the other. The altar boy on the right was responsible for ringing the bells during the Consecration and other ceremonies. It pretty much went off without a hitch, though I messed up a little in my journey with the big book, taking the wrong route from one side of the altar to the other. Not bad for the first time.

The best part about serving Mass was how cool you looked in the robes. At St. John's, you wore a long red tunic that snapped down the front and went all the way to the floor. Then you put on this big white shirt that had a square opening at the top so you could see the red underneath.

Every once in a while, you got to do a funeral and wear a black robe underneath the white. That was even better.

One of the other things that was great about being an altar boy was being late for school when you had a weekday morning Mass. Sometimes, there were two Masses in a row if one of the other priests had to get his in as well. Not only could you waltz into class late, but you were allowed to cross Dixwell Avenue after Mass and spend a few minutes having breakfast at The Donut Shop. Fred Starno, Tom Smith or Rob Caron would often join me for glazed donuts and chocolate eclairs for twenty minutes or so before we crossed back to school.

A year or two later, Monsignor Donnely was promoted to Bishop, and that was a big deal from an altar boy standpoint. He got to have his hands washed twice and every time he gave a blessing, he had to make the Sign of the Cross three times. He also got a great big ring we were supposed to kiss, but Bishop Donnely didn't seem to go in for that.

My newfound position didn't stop me from riding my bike up to Al's Superette, looking for the first series of baseball cards. I don't know if it was my age, my fascination with The Beatles or my interest in girls, but the anticipation wasn't quite the same. If I had fifteen cents, instead of buying three packs of cards, I might only buy one pack and use the rest to buy Cheese Twists. Jimmy and I would then ride back to my house and head down to the woods. We would spend the afternoon eating our snacks and discussing the girls in class.

That season was also my second year playing baseball for Hamden Plaza. Some of the other eleven year olds had now moved up to the Majors too, so there were more friends on my team. I remember an ugly scene on Opening Day when a kid's father came into the dugout and began arguing with our coach, Mr. Downs, about his son not playing enough. Mr. Downs tried to stay calm, but the man just worked himself into a rage. Right in front of all of us, the father began screaming and swearing at our coach. A couple of the parents had to run in and restrain him, and that made the guy even wilder. No one got hurt, but it put a damper on the game.

It was a big year for me in baseball. We had a twelve year old on our team, Jay Mitchell, who was a fantastic ball player. He was also a great guy and the leader of our team. He batted fourth while I batted third. I got a ton of hits that year, and it seemed like every time I was on base, Jay would step up to the plate and blast one over the left-field fence. He was also an intimidating pitcher, great speed and a little wild, while I was handling the shortstop position pretty well. We were winning most of our games, and the town weekly newspaper, *The Hamden Chronicle*, once referred to us as "The local M and M Boys," for Mitchell and Murphy. Jay and I made the All Star team that year. I enjoyed the celebrity status, but Jay was the main man.

That summer, my family and I went down to New York City to attend the World's Fair. Grandma Vivian came along, too. It was bigger and better than any amusement park I had ever seen. I especially liked any exhibit where you sat on a moving chair and were taken on a journey of some kind. The ones that left the biggest impression on me were General Electric, General Motors, Bell Telephone and the Ford Exhibit.

The Ford Exhibit was great because you were actually able to get inside one of the new Mustangs, and it took you on an educational voyage.

It was soon time for our summer vacation, and my parents had to figure out what we were going to do now that Cape Cod would never be the same without President Kennedy. We ended up going into upstate New York and over the border into Canada. It was supposed to be an "educational" trip with stops at Fort Ticonderoga, The Plains of Abraham and then down to the Amish country in Lancaster, Pennsylvania. I guess it was fairly educational, but we still managed to have a great vacation. We even spent a couple of days at Niagara Falls and took the Maid of the Mist boat right to where the water came crashing down. We all had to wear raincoats for that.

In Canada, my parents decided to get pretty religious and we had to go to a bunch of shrines up there. I remember climbing about a hundred stairs on my knees in order to buy a ten-thousand year indulgence. That meant if you went to Purgatory and had a sentence of 150,000 years, 10,000 were automatically knocked off because you made it up those stairs. There were also a lot of people in wheel chairs looking for miracles. I remember one night when we all had to hold a lighted candle and march around another shrine, forming a sort of human rosary. That looked pretty cool.

The best part of the trip was toward the end when we headed down to Lancaster County to see the Amish people. I couldn't believe there were people still living without electricity, television or telephones. They were still getting around with horses and carriages and dressed like people from the 19th Century. The biggest impression on me were kids living that way. They looked so good in their hats and bonnets. We stopped at a number of homes and bought fresh vegetables from their roadside stands.

I remember not being able to find a decent motel and getting a little nervous about finding a couple of rooms for the night, when we found a place called the Host Motel. It turned out to be a beautiful motel, and they were able to squeeze us in. We enjoyed it there so much that we stayed a couple of extra days. There was an enormous swimming pool with a number of high diving boards and even a big platform that might have been thirty feet high. Howie and I had a ball doing dives and cannon balls. We even met some kids there our age. The Host Motel was the highlight of the vacation.

By the middle of August, we would occasionally have one of those really crisp mornings when you needed to wear a sweatshirt. That was the first indication that summer was ending and it was time to start thinking about school again. As usual, we savored those last few days.

Chapter Eight

1964–1965

Stepping Out

Seventh grade began in September. Our teacher was Mother St. Laura, a tall, quiet and almost saintly nun. Some of the wise guys in class took advantage of her demeanor, and I remember those first few weeks being loud and chaotic. Mother St. Laura must have had some personal problems, because she would be missing for several weeks at a time, come back for a while, and then be gone again. It turned out to be a year of substitutes for our class.

That fall, Jimmy Reardon and I came up with a terrific new game at a place between our homes known as The Meadow. Unlike the bean fields on my side of the woods, The Meadow was bright green grass with lots of milk weeds and cat o nine tails. A year earlier, we had found a collection of bones there that Jimmy identified as dinosaur remains. For a couple of days, we thought we were going to be rich and famous for finding these fossils. However, when we brought a couple into school, we were told that they were from steaks and pork chops.

The game we invented in The Meadow featured the digging of deep and narrow holes in the ground along one of the main paths. They were about a foot in diameter but went down almost two feet. Somehow, the soil there was perfect for digging. Once we dug about ten or fifteen holes, we'd cover them up with weeds and straw we found. Next came the really smart part. We would race down the trail as fast as we could, one at a time, to see how far we could get before being upended by one of the hidden "traps." It's a miracle that we played this game for about three weeks without breaking a leg.

I started to serve Mass more and more in the seventh grade. I remember a couple of Masses in the middle of the week when I would start to feel lousy up on the altar. There was that awful feeling of not knowing whether or not you were going to throw up, and not wanting to leave your post. You also didn't want the world to know you were sick so you would go through a miserable time for several minutes trying to decide whether or not you should leave. On one occasion, it got so bad that I just couldn't kneel any more at the altar, so instead of leaving the area, I simply turned around, faced the congregation, and sat on the marble steps like I was on a curb. Father Kevin turned around to look at me. He whispered, "Murph, are you all right?" I nodded my head and waved for him to keep saying the Mass. Joseph Valla was on the Bells side that morning, and I thought he was going to die, holding in his laughter. After Mass, Father Kevin told me to leave the altar the next time I felt sick.

There was one altar boy who used to say the earliest Sunday morning Mass, 7:00 a.m. Maybe he didn't have time for breakfast, I don't know, but he would faint now and then during the sermon. You would figure that he would be given another Mass, but Tom Smith said the priests noticed the big increase in attendance and were making more money at the 7:00 collection. I wasn't sure about that.

I was at the time a big fan of football. I had been to several major league baseball games but had never been to a real football game at any level. Finally, Mom and Dad decided it was time to spend a Saturday afternoon at the Yale Bowl in New Haven. I had been by there a hundred times before, but it was not that impressive from the outside. Inside, however, was a different story. It was spacious and imposing.

That day, we saw Columbia play against Yale, but it was not what I expected. First of all, Columbia had light blue jerseys, and Yale had navy blue jerseys. I had never seen a football game on TV where one team did not wear white. Dad explained that one team normally wore white when the game was televised, so people could tell the difference between the players on their black and white sets. It didn't matter when there was no television coverage. Maybe so, but it didn't look right. The other thing was that the crowd was very quiet. I was expecting lots of noise and cheering. The area we sat in seemed to be made up of professors and doctors. It was a fun day but somewhat of a letdown.

A few weeks later, Dad took the family up to Weslyan University in Middletown where his cousin's son was a football player. His name was Warrie Thomas, and I had only met him once before up in Massachusetts. He was sort of a hero to me because he had let Howie and me ride in his convertible when we visited his family. He was probably ten years older than me, and I was his biggest fan that day. This game was a hundred times more exciting than the Yale game.

Warrie's team was dressed in white jerseys and it played another college dressed in purple. That was more like it. Also, the "stadium" was tiny compared to Yale Bowl, but the noise and excitement on our side of the field were everything I had hoped for and more. The icing on the cake was the fact that Warrie was the hero of the game, a running back barreling over people and flying down the field into the end zone at least a couple of times. We got to walk down on the field after the game, and I met several of Warrie's teammates who went out of their way to be nice to me. Warrie's face was all chewed up, and there was blood on his uniform, too. It was perfect.

Every once in a while, some neighborhood tough kids would slip into the St. John's schoolyard and create a scene. Funny enough, the most threatening one of the bunch was the smallest, a kid named Bobby. He was an eleven-year-old juvenile delinquent. He would come into the schoolyard, openly smoking, swearing like a trooper. He would laugh at the nuns when they tried to throw him out. That kid scared us to death. I never saw him actually hurt anybody, but the humiliation factor was even worse when he would start in on a bigger boy. I never saw anyone stand up to him.

Meanwhile, on weekends, we were still spending most Saturday afternoons at Grandma Vivian's and Sunday afternoons at Grandma Murphy's. On the way home from Ansonia every Saturday night, we would go by West Haven, a shore town, and eat at a place called "Jimmie's of Savin

Rock." It was a drive-in that was packed every night. Everybody in the family but me would usually order a couple of hot dogs with french fries, with coffee for Mom and Dad and hot chocolates for the kids. I always got the lobster roll. On bitter cold winter nights, we would watch a skin form over the top of the hot chocolate, and for added entertainment, we would write our names and play tic tac toe on the fogged-up windows.

If we were good in the car, my father would drive us across the street to Carvel for ice cream cones. This was a very busy road and my father had to be very, very careful crossing from Jimmie's parking lot to Carvel. He would always ask the same question as he slowly inched out, "How's it your way?" After Mom gave him clearance, he would move the Impala into the street. One night, I decided to have a little fun at Dad's expense. I elbowed Howie and whispered, "Watch this!"

Just as he started to ease the car slowly into the road, I quietly sneaked up behind him from the back seat. He checked both ways, and as usual, asked my mother, "How's it your way?" A couple of seconds later, he accelerated, and the car started moving into the road. At that instant, I yelled, "Look Out!" as loud as I could. Dad jammed on the brakes, making a screeching noise. Everything in the car went flying. I mean everything. Coffee, hot chocolate, paper plates and my little sister, Maureen. Well, I didn't get an ice cream that night. It also hurt to sit down for a couple of days.

Dad wasn't in good spirits at that time, but he had his moments. I loved when we would get him talking about his younger days. He had graduated from Manhattan College in the Spring of 1942 and joined the Army Air Force. Once in a while, we would find some old pictures up in the attic and would get him telling us all about his experiences in World War II. He served in England, mostly a desk job, but had some great pictures and stories of the German bombers hitting his base each night.

I think I had the only father who would often say "World War II was one of the best times of my life. I was in the best shape ever, I had plenty of good food to eat, I had great friends, and I had two pairs of comfortable shoes." There's a lesson in there somewhere.

The life of a soldier must have interested me. One day, the family took a ride up to West Point, New York, to visit the military academy. I was pretty familiar with the place and all its traditions because there was a TV show Howie and I used to watch called *The West Point Story*. I don't think it was on the air very long but it was one of our favorites. Anyway, I was captivated by all the cadets walking around, saluting and marching in the parades. There was also enough girl watching to keep me happy. Plenty of beautiful girls were up there visiting the cadets. It seemed like a perfect place to spend four years. For several weeks afterward, I felt sure I wanted to be a West Point student someday.

Back at St. John's, things were pretty much the same. Once you got to seventh grade, however, you had the privilege of being able to check out the most popular book from the school library, *The Good Bad Boy*. This was the only book where there was actually a waiting list. I got it several times in seventh and eighth grade and I pretty much read it from cover to cover in a couple of days each time. It was a diary of a boy growing up in the eighth grade. The book had it all: nuns, sports, girlfriends, rivals, and more. There was even one part where he got into serious trouble when one of the parish priests saw him smoking a cigarette. What a great book.

Some of my other favorites were *The Babe Ruth Story, Francis Marion, Mad Anthony Wayne* and *Simon Kenton.* These books dealt primarily with the childhood of famous people. I also picked up a terrific book at the annual book fair called *The Civil War.* It had tons of pictures and maps. It became my favorite book to read when I was eating cereal every night.

That year, I finally saved up enough money to get my own Beatles album. Even though it had been out for a while, I had to have the *Beatles' Second Album.* This record had the song *You Can't Do That.* I don't know how many times I listened to those songs. Often I would lie on the floor next to the big hi-fi and swing my head, just like Paul and George swung their heads into the microphone to sing harmony. I didn't just listen, I studied every bit of each song. My other favorite cuts from the album were *Thank You Girl, I'll Get You* and *Devil In Her Heart.*

I was starting to make some money after snow storms by shoveling driveways and sidewalks in the neighborhood. One day, we woke up to about a foot of snow, and I spent the entire day shoveling out several of the homes in the neighborhood. I made a small fortune.

That night, Dad came home much later than usual. He had walked a few miles home after his car got stuck in the snow somewhere between his office and our house. He was not in great spirits to begin with, but I guess he noticed the fact that every house in the neighborhood was shoveled out except for the Murphy's. It didn't get much better when the next thing he saw was me sitting in the warm living room, dollar bills stacked everywhere while I counted my loot. I think I was up until 11 o'clock that night shoveling our own driveway and sidewalk.

Every once in a while, there would be a reason for the family to go to downtown New Haven. To get there, we went through the section where the "colored people" lived. The only Black person I knew was a girl in my class named Theresa Thimpson. She was very quiet and was one of the smartest kids in the class.

I couldn't understand why they all seemed to live in one place. I also couldn't understand why it looked so much more interesting than where I lived. There seemed to be a hundred times more activity. Grownups and children were everywhere. They were coming in and out of stores, standing around and talking. They all seemed to be enjoying themselves. It was a totally different world. I just couldn't understand why there were two separate ones.

Jimmy Reardon and I were now twelve years old and were beginning to explore other areas further from our homes. Far past the woods and the bean fields, there was a sand quarry with big dunes going down into what was thought of as a "bottomless lake." This was considered a very dangerous area, and we had heard stories of people over the years drowning in it. We started to spend some time skipping rocks across the lake and jumping off the sand dunes. On the other side of the quarry was the dreaded Brookside, so we always had to keep our eyes open for those kids.

About a quarter of a mile up from the quarry was a fantastic area that looked like the heart of the country. This was called Montevani's Land. There were apple orchards, farm equipment and old sheds everywhere. Plus, there were constant rumors of Old Man Montevani roaming his land with a shot gun. Many of the big kids told stories of being shot with rock salt or being chased by Montevani's blood-thirsty dogs. However, the beauty of the area and the danger that went with it were too much of a temptation for us to stay away. It seemed like a million miles away from our neighborhood.

Up from Montevani's land were the enormous cliffs that belonged to Blakeslee Concrete. For years and years, Blakeslee would blast the rock out of the cliffs. You could often hear the explosions from miles away. Jimmy and I would sometimes approach the cliffs from behind and suddenly, there was a spectacular sight for us. We could see the entire skyline of New Haven several miles away, New Haven Harbor entering into Long Island Sound, and on a clear day, even the coast of Long Island, New York far off in the distance. Way down below us were the Blakeslee workers, looking like ants going about their jobs.

What I remember most about the quarry, Montevani's land and the Blakeslee cliffs was lying in bed at night. I would often think how glad I was to be in my safe house, in my bed, and not in those dangerous areas. I would always tell myself that I would never go up there again. But in the daytime, those places didn't seem so bad, and they kept drawing us to them.

The morning routine on school days consisted of getting up, having about four pieces of toast with peanut butter, getting ready for school and watching TV about a half an hour before the bus came. For years, we would settle in to enjoy *The Little Rascals*. I saw each episode at least fifty times and could recite every line of every kid from Chubbie to Jackie to Spanky and Alfalfa. I still feel that those old shows were classics.

At night, my new favorite show was *Daniel Boone*, starring Fess Parker. He played the same type of role he had as Davy Crockett in the Walt Disney show. I think this was an hour episode and I loved it when it was tied into American History. Every once in a while there would be someone on the show that I had read about. I liked his daughter a lot, too.

It was also about this time that our family was enjoying a TV show called *The King Family Hour.* This was something similar to the *Osmond Show* of the 70s. The King Family must have had about fifty relatives or so, all of whom could play instruments and sing. We knew most of them by name and followed them closely. My favorites were the King cousins. They were a few blond teenage girls who sang some of the latest pop tunes. The most popular one was Tina Cole. She ended up joining the cast of *My Three Sons* as Robbie's wife.

That spring, we started to get ready for baseball season again, and I was excited about the chance to play for two teams. Hamden Plaza was moving to another league, so I was going to join either the Hamden Barbers or Al Porto & Sons. I was hoping to join Al Porto because Billy Garcia from across the street was on that team. I was thrilled when I got the news that the team had picked me.

I also was trying out for Saint John the Baptist. Father Frisbee was the coach of this team, and it was baseball at a more advanced level. The bases were the full ninety feet apart, leading was permitted and you got to wear real metal spikes. It didn't look like I had made the team until one of the regular players broke his arm.

The best part about playing for Saint John's was game day. Right in front of the entire class, a few of us got to stand up about two o'clock and head to the bathrooms where we changed into our full dress uniforms. Then we got to come back to class and stay there about ten or fifteen minutes before we were off again to do battle for Saint John's. Being in that classroom in that uniform was quite the ego trip. I really felt like a big celebrity, especially in front of the girls.

My St. John's career didn't get off to the best of starts. In one early game, I remember being on second base with nobody out. Not being used to leading off the base, I noticed that the pitcher was going into a full windup instead of the usual half-stretch motion to keep me close to the bag. I looked over at third base and there seemed to be a lot of people in that area: third baseman, third base coach, and an umpire. Unfortunately, what I did not see was my teammate, Gary Thibideau, ten or fifteen feet down the line from third. I was thrilled to think that the pitcher had forgotten I was on second base and decided that if he was foolish enough to go into the full stretch again, I would be off like a flash and into third base, no problem. Was he going to be embarrassed! On the next pitch, I saw the full stretch again and not believing my good luck, streaked into third base, performing a perfect slide and popping right up and into the bag with no throw! I stood there brushing off the dirt from my pants when I looked up into the disbelieving eyes of Gary. I quickly decided that I had no business being there and made a beeline back to second base. Meanwhile, Gary sprinted towards home plate where he was thrown out easily. Not one of my better moments on the diamond.

Of all the people I had to do that to, Gary Thibideau was the coolest of the cool. He was a good student, had one of the prettiest girlfriends, was captain of the altar boys and captain of the baseball team. The tough kids accepted him as one of their own even though he never got into any trouble. He simply commanded respect wherever he went. He never picked on anybody, and no one ever picked on him. This kid had it all.

Memorial Day was one of the best holidays of the year. Hamden had a great big parade that started at the First National Grocery Store on Dixwell Avenue and moved all the way up to Hamden High School. As members of organized baseball, we got to walk as a team all the way up Dixwell Avenue in the parade. This is something we looked forward to for weeks. As each team walked under the Benham Street bridge at the end of the parade route, we would chant out our cheer, listening to the echoes around us. That was a tradition for years.

Memorial Day was also the first "official" day of summer and the first day we were allowed to go swimming up at Paradise Park, a great place we enjoyed for years and years. Paradise Park had a swimming pool, a swimming pond, another lake for boating and fishing, a baseball field, tennis courts and picnic areas. Many of the families in the Furman Road area belonged to Paradise, and the weekends were always the best. We would pack a cooler full of sodas and hamburgers to cook that evening. There was nothing better than that cookout after a day of swimming and baseball. At the end of the meal, we would always find some good sticks to roast marshmallows on. It was great to be with all the neighborhood kids and their parents. It was always a little strange from Memorial Day until school got out in the middle of June. It didn't seem right to have to think about school on Monday morning when you were having that much fun on Sunday night.

At the beginning of June each year, I went to Lake Quasapaug for the Saint John's altar boy picnic. As in other matters, Jimmy Reardon and I would plot out our strategy for weeks before the big event. We would spend the entire day riding the Wild Mouse, the Octopus and the Twister. I remember that every year it was a perfect sunny day for the altar boy picnic. I was absolutely convinced that God was taking care of us for all the work we had done serving Mass during the year.

Going home on the bus at night was always the same feeling. You felt like you were still on the rides. A lot of times we would break out into songs on the way home.

I had my best year playing baseball for Al Porto, but something was beginning to change for me. I found myself really enjoying the games while I was playing, but worrying about them all day before the 6:00 p.m. start. I don't know why that was, maybe it was because I was expected to perform better. But I remember looking forward to days that I didn't have a game that night. I couldn't figure that out. I mean this was baseball for twelve year olds. What was the big deal? I should have just enjoyed the competition, done my best and had fun. I really liked Saturdays after we had played and especially if I had played well. I'd love to hang around the field for hours afterward, watching the other games and knowing I had done my job. It was almost a relief that the game was over.

Jimmy Reardon and his family moved at the end of the school year. They had a new house in the northern part of Hamden called Mount Carmel, way up on West Woods Road. He was going to live several miles away from me and although he would go back to Saint John's for eighth grade, I knew it was going to be different. It wasn't such a big deal for the summer, because I always sort of switched friends for the summer during grammar school. Billy Garcia and I hung around together, which usually centered around whiffle ball for hours in the morning and Paradise Park in the afternoon.

The Knights of Columbus is a large Catholic fraternal organization that had maybe one and a half million men as members. It was founded by a priest in New Haven in the 1880s. That summer, the whole family was going to join Dad at their annual convention. His whole career was with the Supreme Headquarters for the Knights of Columbus in New Haven and he had risen through the ranks in different management and executive positions. Every August, he went away for one of these big trips. Now it was time for all of us to go with him.

The convention of 1965 was in Baltimore, and we were going to go for the whole thing. I wasn't sure what to expect or even what a convention was, and I remember hearing a lot of lectures about how important it was for us kids to be on our best behavior since there were a lot of important people there. But later we learned of the activities that they had for the children at the convention, including bus trips, Washington DC tours and even teenage dances at night. I was twelve years old, going on thirteen, so I was going to be allowed to go to these teenage functions.

We drove down to Baltimore and, right in the middle of the downtown area, checked into an old building called the Lord Baltimore Hotel. I had never been in a tall building like that before and I probably spent a couple of hours going up and down every elevator, stopping at every floor. There were restaurants everywhere, a great balcony on the second floor which looked into the lobby and thousands of people.

Dad had to arrive at the convention several days before it began to be part of the preparations, so I got to watch him in action when I ran into him those first few days. Although I didn't know it at the time, of course, I really learned a lot watching Dad greet all the attendees, including all the various levels of the clergy. I also learned just who each of the top people were at the Knights of Columbus. Every one of them went out of his way to shake hands and visit with me for a while.

Over those first few days, more and more people would show up, signs and banners would begin to appear, and there was a terrific anticipation of the events to come. After we had been there a couple of days, Dad told Howie and me that we were going to be going to a Baltimore Orioles baseball game that evening with a man and his sons from Kansas. The father's name was Virgil Dechant, and his two older sons were Tommy who was my age, and his younger brother, Danny. I wasn't sure about making a new friend, but at least Howie was going to be with me. Naturally, I was excited about seeing a new ballpark.

That night, we got into one of the Knights of Columbus courtesy cars and were driven to Memorial Stadium. We had fantastic seats. There was a rain delay in the middle of the game, and it was fun to watch the stadium crew cover the field.

Tommy Dechant and I hit it off from the beginning, and I spent the rest of the convention running around with him. What a thrill it was for both of us to eat to our heart's content at every meal and simply sign our fathers' names and room numbers to the bills. We lived like kings for a whole week.

Tommy and I ended up becoming pen pals and wrote to each other regularly over the next year, eagerly awaiting the next convention and then the one after that. I got to go to some really wonderful places: Miami Beach, Montreal, Disneyland in California and Houston. These conventions turned out to be about the best vacations a young teenager could ask for.

The letters that Tommy and I would exchange usually discussed baseball and girls. As we got older, the letters moved toward current events and girls.

I also got pretty friendly with a boy from Canada who attended these conventions, Joey. He hung around with Tommy and me, and I remember him giving me some tips for our first teenage dance. I pretty much thought that we would be doing the Cha-Cha and Fox Trot I had learned from William's Ballroom Studio. I then learned that people were doing things like the Jerk, so I needed some quick training. I practiced and practiced that afternoon and finally felt I was ready for the big event.

That night I went to my first teenage dance. I saw a pretty girl. Somehow asking her to dance was a lot harder than three years earlier at dancing school. I probably wasted half the night staring at her and trying to gather up the courage to approach. She had long, brown, wavy hair and gorgeous eyes. Every time I thought I was close to walking over to her, another guy would dance with her. Finally, I figured that no matter how embarrassing it would be if she said, "no," it was worth trying. Who knows, she might say, "yes." Wasn't the chance of dancing with her worth the risk? I probably repeated that question to myself a hundred times over the next few years. Anyway, with my heart pounding and my palms sweating, I moved in on her. Without thinking, I resorted back to my formal dancing school days and asked her, "May I please have this dance?" I didn't mean to sound so formal, but she smiled at me and shook her head, "yes." We went out onto the dance floor and I put my newly discovered moves to the music. I probably looked like something out of a Jerry Lewis movie but I felt pretty hip.

After the fast dance ended, the band went right into a slow one. Feeling pretty confident now and getting rid of the nervous jitters, I asked her if she wanted to dance again. She smiled and moved into my arms. This dance was a heck of a lot different than the waltzes I had done at the age of nine. As a matter of fact, it really wasn't dancing at all and still was more fun than anything else I had ever done in my life. All you had to do was put your arms around her lower back while she put hers around your neck, then simply move back and forth to the beat of the music. We spent the rest of the dance together, and I remember buying her a couple of Cokes. Her name was Karen, and her family was at their first convention, too.

The week began winding down, and I remember the incredible letdown of watching the people checking out in the lobby. Everyone was saying "see you in Miami," but that seemed to be an eternity away. I was also already missing Karen and I probably didn't get over her for at least a week. That convention was the best vacation I had ever had. Fortunately, all the other ones I was to go to were just as good.

By the time we got home, it was just a matter of a few days before school started. I was ready to start my final year at St. John the Baptist.

Chapter Nine

1965–1966

Growing Up with The Boston Strangler

*E*ighth grade, Mother Saint Catherine. We were now the oldest kids at Saint John's, but it was a little unusual not having Jimmy Reardon living near me. Every once in a while, I'd go to his house and spend the weekend, but it was never the same.

That fall, Howie was a Senior at Notre Dame High School, and our family took a few trips up through New England to look at colleges for him. This was pretty boring to me in the back seat. My father had the World Series going all the time on the car radio, but it didn't mean much. For the first time that I could ever recall, the Yankees were not in it.

We saw Boston College, Stonehill College, Saint Anselm's and Saint Michael's. One of the priests at Saint Anselm's had died a couple of days before one of our trips and, for some reason, we all stopped off at the chapel to pay our respects. I got to see another dead body, but other than that, it was very boring.

Back at home, I was spending most of my free time down in the finished-off basement, still pounding ping-pong balls against the wall and watching television. Some of my new favorite shows were *Petticoat Junction* and *Gilligan's Island.* I loved when *Petticoat Junction* would have some of the cast of *The Beverly Hillbillies* appear on it. I always thought that was so clever. My favorite sister of the three girls was always the middle one, Bobby Joe. I thought she was the best looking of the bunch, but it seemed that the older sister, Billy Joe, and the younger sister, Betty Joe, got most of the attention. I was also fascinated on how the actress who played Kate was also the voice of Betty in the Flinstones.

Howie and I would save our best debates for *Gilligan's Island:* who was better, Mary Anne or Ginger? His girl was Mary Anne, mine was Ginger. I guess he liked the more wholesome type of girl, but I know what I liked, too, even at the age of 13.

My father loved any situation comedy that had a military theme. He would sit and roar at *Gomer Pyle, USMC* and *McHale's Navy.* I used to love watching Captain Binghamton go through his antics, just to see my father laughing. *F-Troop* would kill him, too.

My brother, Howie, and his friends always seemed to be doing something much more interesting than what I was used to. One time, Howie, Paul Keating, Myles Moran, Frank Sarvillo, John Ditta, Billy Grant and some others were challenged by some other guys to a big game of tackle football. They spent a couple of weeks clearing out a section of the bean field to make it into an official football field. They even found an old decoration float over at Southern Connecticut State College and brought it over. After all that effort, they must have been short a person, so I was invited to be the eleventh man. Needless to say, I was thrilled. We practiced most afternoons and evenings for a week but seemed to spend more time working on how we would run out of the woods (our locker room) and into the bean field before the game. I was pretty good at that part.

The following Sunday was Game Day, but after Mass, I learned that the whole thing was falling through. None of the older guys seemed to care very much and began making plans on what to do for the rest of the day. As for me, I had had it in my mind that this was going to be as big as any NFL championship and was absolutely heartbroken when it didn't happen. I couldn't understand how all that work and preparation went for nothing.

During the school week, our normal meals were steak, pork chops, stew, pot roast, breaded veal cutlets, ham, and on Fridays, eggs or fish. One day, my mother found out she was a little bit anemic and needed to eat liver every couple of weeks. The arguing and fighting were unbelievable. You couldn't leave the table until you finished that disgusting meat. I often managed to stuff the pieces into my pockets and flush them down the toilet after dinner. My father would go to the bathroom right after me. I think he was doing the same thing.

Sunday meals began to change. We had had big dinners for years, but now, going out to Sunday breakfast was the latest rage. Depending on what Mass I was serving, we would head down the Merit Parkway to go to a Howard Johnson's or go to the International House of Pancakes where there was usually a ten or fifteen minute wait. I liked this place the best because you could get lunch or breakfast. It didn't matter. I always went with "Our Own Hamburger" or a ham omelet.

Vietnam came to our school that year. A girl in our class lost her brother, and there was a big funeral Mass that we all attended. I knew nothing about this place called Vietnam and had no idea what the war was about. All I remember is sitting and staring at that flag-draped casket, which reminded me of what had happened to John Kennedy a couple of years earlier. The girl and her family were crying and holding each other. A few of the girls from our class were also pretty shaken up. I don't think I went through one day in the next several years that the name "Vietnam" didn't come up somehow.

One time, I got pretty sick with bronchitis and I had one of those high fevers that Mom watched closely. I had already been out of school a couple of days and was lying on the "sick couch" one night when the lights went out. We looked outside and saw that there was no power in the rest of the neighborhood. We got the candles out and waited for the power to go back on. Mom started to get worried because she was convinced I might catch pneumonia if the house got too cold. It turned out that this was the famous Eastern Seaboard Blackout. Grandma Vivian called the house and told us that she thought it was the fault of the Russians. The newspaper eventually said that there was a dramatic increase in the number of births exactly nine months after the blackout.

Soon, I was back to my rambunctious self and back at school. Any time in the schoolyard when two boys would start shoving each other, a big circle would form and everyone would start yelling, "fight, fight!" It rarely escalated into punches, but you could usually tell who "won." Not many things bothered me as much as watching the weaker person getting pushed around. The worst case I remember was when a boy in my class, Michael, was being picked on by a boy who was probably four years younger than us but had the reputation of being a tough guy. He started picking on Michael, and the usual crowd gathered. Michael had no idea how to fight back and was quickly put on the ground by the younger boy. I'll never forget that sight of Michael being held down around his shoulders by the other kid's knees and getting slapped lightly on his face and head. It wasn't his physical pain that got to me, but the humiliation in his eyes. Nobody helped Michael; everyone just laughed. I wanted to kill that little kid or at least pull him off Michael but I just walked away from the two of them. If there's any justice, Michael is happy and successful somewhere.

I guess I was pretty lucky along those lines. The tough kids in my class were always friendly to me. Maybe it was because I could hold my own with them in sports. I had been playing baseball with them for the last three years. The few times I did have to fight were occasioned by my being pushed too far. And I usually just flailed away until it was over. Howie had always taught me to not stop punching and always throw everything at your opponent's nose. That always brought blood and, usually, tears.

Now that we were big eighth graders, sometimes the nuns would let Tommy Smith and me walk down to Freddy Starno's house, which was just a couple of hundred yards from the schoolyard, and join him for lunch. Freddy's father had an old National Geographic's black and white movie that lasted about twenty minutes. The three of us would put the reels together then sit throughout the entire boring movie, watching native dances and a lion hunt.

Why? Because in the last fifteen seconds of the movie, there was a victory dance where all the native women were naked. Unfortunately, we couldn't freeze or rewind the movie, so we studied those few seconds at the end very closely. We rarely had time to eat our sandwiches.

In March of 1966, it was time to take the entrance exam to Notre Dame High School. I never considered going anywhere else. One Saturday morning, I had to go there and take tests for about four hours. I found out a couple of months later that I had been accepted, along with about seven or eight other guys from St. John's. That was a big deal.

The day I took the entrance exam, I received a phone call from Mrs. Gorman, who lived around the corner from us. She wanted to know if I would take care of cutting her grass all spring and summer. She was going to pay me three dollars a week and supply the lawn mower. I didn't like the idea of having to take on any responsibilities that might interfere with my doing nothing. However, my parents insisted, so I took the job. Unfortunately, Mrs. Gorman's lawn mower was not the gasoline-powered kind, but rather one of those electric Sunbeam models, with a long cord. It was a total pain trying to get around trees and bushes with that cord. I ended up cutting her grass for the next three years. I always hated to go over there, but always loved it when I sat down with a cold Coca-Cola after the job was completed.

I played baseball again for Saint John the Baptist but announced my retirement from the Hamden Fathers' Baseball League. I was now old enough to go into the Babe Ruth League but I remembered how I felt about organized baseball a year earlier and really didn't want to play. I know my parents were disappointed and I got tired of answering the same question from everyone I ran into, "Why aren't you playing ball this year?" I really didn't have a good answer. I just didn't want any part of it. In looking back, I guess I didn't want any part of responsibilities, even organized baseball. Ten years later, I absolutely lived for organized softball.

That spring, another fad came around, but this one would last to this day: Frisbees. I bought one, bright blue, and played with it constantly. Surprisingly, there were not many people who could throw the thing properly. They always had a knack of "hooking" it so it would nose-dive from left to right. I had little patience with people who couldn't throw it properly and still do. It seems like such a simple thing.

We also bought another new car that spring, a 1966 Chevy Chevelle. This one was red, and it was the first car we ever owned that had seat belts. For some reason, this new car wasn't nearly as exciting as when we bought the '64 Impala. I didn't even go with my parents to bring it home. We finally got rid of the old blue and white Chevy that was now twelve years old. I kind of hated to see that one go. So many of my best memories were in that old car.

Every spring, Notre Dame High School would put on this big musical production called the Spring Festival. It was really quite a show, considering it was all high school students. The girls in the Spring Festival were all from Notre Dame's sister school in Hamden, a private girls high school call Sacred Heart Academy. Howie was in the Glee Club for four years and was part of the Spring Festival. It ran all week, but the biggest night was the finale, Saturday night. The scenery and the costumes were always fantastic, and the girls always looked beautiful. That year, I remember some of the girls in a carnival setting riding on swings and flying way out high over the audience. While this was going on, a bunch of other girls came down the aisle from the back of the auditorium, riding on wooden merry-go-round horses. One of the main stars went right past my seat, smiling and waving to everyone.

Soon after that Spring Festival was over, we read in the paper one morning that three of these girls from Sacred Heart Academy were killed in a terrible automobile accident in Hamden the night before. It turns out my brother knew them all, as well as a couple of others who were critically injured. The Sacred Heart girls had been heading down the Merit Parkway when another driver somehow jumped the narrow median and soared up into the air and down, head-on into the car carrying them. It's all everybody talked about for the next week. It had a big impact on me. They had looked so beautiful a few days earlier. Now, just like that, they were gone. For a long time, I hated driving on any big highway. I couldn't imagine what it was like to be in an accident like that.

I guess that some things just really got to me, big time. For instance, that year, a bunch of nursing students out in Chicago were brutally murdered by a man who had broken into their apartment. They caught the guy pretty quick, Richard Speck. I read everything in the newspaper that had to do with that crime. One of the girls had spent the whole night hiding under a bed, while the killer kept coming into the room and taking out one girl at a time to kill her. The thought of that nurse hiding all night that way really bothered me. Why were there things like that happening in our world? And did it bother other eighth graders as much as it bothered me?

About the same time, we started hearing about some housewives in Hamden and a couple of neighboring towns who had been attacked and molested by some guy known simply as *the green man*. This was even worse than the Richard Speck murders because this guy had not yet been caught, and he had been in my town. He disguised himself as a repairman with dark green overalls, hence the nickname. That man gave me a few sleepless nights. A long time later, someone told me that they caught the guy, and he turned out to be someone named Albert DeSalvo, better known as the Boston Strangler. I'm not sure if that was true.

Around that time, Howie was ending his Senior year in high school and had been accepted to Manhattan College down in New York City, my father's alma mater. Howie seemed to have so many things going on which, in my eyes, looked great. When he had a date on a Friday night, I was so envious. I wished it was me doing all the things he got to do. Lots of times, his friends would be at our house, and I would have to walk that fine line of being close to the action, but not so involved I would risk banishment by Howie.

One of the funniest things I ever saw was when he and his friends got hold of a movie camera and made an epic film called *Lassie Gets a New Tractor.* They had everything: overalls, corn cob pipes, a pickup truck and cardboard signs to show the dialogue. Howie played the part of Gramps; Paul Keating was Timmy; his sister, Chris, was June; Joe Lecza was her husband; and Gerard Nutcher played the part of Lassie. I was even given a cameo role as

Doc, the local veterinarian. One my favorite scenes was when Gramps told Timmy and some of his playmates to get their chores done, and they all suddenly attacked him, beating him to a pulp. Great fun. That movie still comes out once in a while today.

I was finishing up at Saint John's, and it was time for the eighth grade picnic at, where else, Lake Quasapaug. Jimmy Reardon and I were fortunate enough to spend the day hanging around with two girls from our class. My girl was Gail Alberino. She was a beauty who spent most of her time with the tough crowd but, for some reason, was with me. A few times, I worked hard and summoned up the courage to put my arm around the back of her seat on one of the rides. I was scared to death but had to do it. I was caught between wanting my fellow eighth graders to see me, but not wanting Gail to see my arm, fearing all kinds of rejection. It was a stress-ful day.

That summer didn't have the same feeling as others gone by. For the last couple of years, the big kids were getting involved in part-time jobs. Now several of them had full-time jobs for the entire summer. Even then, I noticed that things couldn't stay the same. Things had a way of moving on. As you got older, there were more and more exciting things to do but with them also came more and more responsibility. Summers weren't the same anymore. When the big kids weren't working, they were out in someone's car for the night.

In August of 1966, it was time for our second Knights of Columbus Convention. This year was to be even better than Baltimore. We were driving down to Miami Beach. The interstates didn't go as far as they do today, so it was going to take three days to get there. The first day, we got all the way to North Carolina. The next day our route seemed to be all back roads, and we didn't make good time at all. However, the best part of this second day was watching all the big billboards for a place called South of the Border. There were advertisements for probably 200 miles. Looking ahead to those signs made a long trip much more bearable. When we finally got closer, the billboards would appear every ten miles, then five miles, then every mile. We didn't stop at South of the Border, but I remember the last billboard about a quarter of a mile past the place, "Backup, Amigo, You Missed It!"

Howie and I got pretty good at singing practically every song we knew during those three days. We would do lots of Beatles' tunes, harmonizing pretty well. We finally arrived in Miami on the third day and checked into the most beautiful hotel I'd ever seen, the Fontainbleau.

This convention was even better than Baltimore. Tom Dechant and I immediately got together and spent the entire week having a terrific time in the ocean and in the swimming pools. Again, we ate like kings and simply signed our hotel room numbers. There were plenty of activities for the teenagers as well, including a couple of dances. Joey, the boy from Canada, joined us, as did a boy from North Haven, Connecticut. His name was Jim Griffin and his father worked at the headquarters with my father. There were about nine or ten kids in his family, which was a fun loving group. We kids had a ball.

As usual, there was a big letdown as the convention began to wind down. The ride back home to Connecticut seemed to take forever. I was still pretty scared about driving fast after the deaths of the Sacred Heart girls. To make it even worse, Dad would often let Howie drive the car. I hated it when he was behind the wheel.

Traveling through the Deep South back then was quite an education. I saw tiny little shacks and kids playing out in front of them. Some of them were selling vegetables on the side of the road. I loved the way they talked. It was like being in a different world. I was always attracted to the South after that trip.

Chapter Ten

1966–1967

High School and More Vietnam

Howie went off to college that fall, and I started Notre Dame High School. My father drove some of my friends and me to school early each morning. He had done this for four years with Howie, and now it was my turn. Notre Dame was about thirty minutes away by car, but it took much longer to get home each afternoon by the public bus system.

A kid who lived a few streets over from me, Steve Hammond, started riding to school with us every morning. He had gone to the public schools prior to that, and I didn't know him too well. He would become one of my closest friends. A boy from St. John's, Billy Dest, also joined us for the ride. Over the years, we eventually squeezed in my old pal, Freddy Starno, and Steve's younger brother, Ronnie.

Notre Dame was pretty imposing for a Freshman. The teachers were clergy members, the Brothers of Holy Cross, a no-nonsense bunch of men who had a reputation for smacking kids first and asking questions later. Changing classes every period was also something new to me. To top it off, there were no girls. I had to wear a jacket and tie, too, but I was used to that.

On the first Friday of school, the Principal announced over the public announcement system to start filing into the gymnasium for something call a "pep rally." I had no idea what this was all about. We were called to the gym by class, Freshmen going last. By the time we started to move over there, I could hear the sound of drums rumbling in the distance. By the time we actually entered the gym, a huge band was playing, too. As soon as the Freshmen walked in, the band stopped, and all the Sophomores, Juniors and Seniors turned in their chairs and bleachers to boo and laugh at us. We had no idea what was going on. It turned out to be some sort of tradition, making fun of the Freshmen. I loved it. After we were finally seated, the cheerleaders started working the crowd into a frenzy with the Notre Dame fight song and other cheers. They had contests to see who could do it the loudest, and, of course, we Freshmen didn't know any of the words. That led to even more booing and laughing. I thought it was wonderful. Suddenly, I got caught up in the Notre Dame tradition and decided I had to go to every football game.

That night, a few of us went to our first high school game. It was under the lights in West Haven, at a place called Quigley Field. I'll never forget the sight of our team, dressed in green and gold and charging out onto the field. It turned out that Notre Dame had a history of great football teams and often won the State Championships. I was hoarse by the end of that game.

During the week, Steve Hammond and I used to walk home from the corner of Dixwell Avenue together. Most days, I ended up going over to his house where we played Stratego for the rest of the afternoon. His parents were pretty strict but always made me feel like a million bucks. I loved going over to Steve's house. We were different in that I had spent much of my childhood playing sports, while he had been involved in Boy Scout-related activities. With Steve, we were always cooking food over a camp fire or building something interesting in his garage.

Completely different than what I had experienced in the eight prior years, Notre Dame of West Haven was an all-boy, Catholic high school that drew "young men" from around the New Haven area. It had a tradition of the finest education and it was also known for its strict order and discipline. The Brothers dressed like priests but couldn't say Mass. They lived in a huge house on the "campus."

Most of the Brothers were pretty nice guys but others had earned the reputation of being extremely tough. Every once in a while, you would see a wise mouth student get slammed up against the lockers or slapped around. I pretty much behaved myself at Notre Dame. One time I got smacked across the head with a textbook for talking in class, but it was nothing too serious.

I'll tell you one thing, there was little trouble with order and discipline in our classes. You couldn't help but concentrate and learn. There was a lot of homework every night, too. Three teachers had the biggest impact on me in my Freshman year, Brother Joseph Lavitto, Brother John Guerriello and Mr. Burg.

Brother Joseph was quite the comedian and really entertained us as he taught. He was the Biology teacher for most students but he also taught a Latin class, and I had him for that. For some reason, he had a pet cat named Ganguffas. He was the mascot in the school, and he walked up and down the aisles of the classroom while Brother Joseph was teaching. The cat climbed in and out of our duffel book bags, stopping at each student to say hello. I loved that class. I did quite well in Latin, memorizing such words as *farmer, poet, Roman soldier, shield, sword,* and *Caesar.* I suppose there were many benefits to taking Latin but I couldn't figure out how many conversations I would have in my life with a gladiator.

Brother John Guerriello was a young man, probably right out of college. He could be pretty funny, too, but there was always a sarcastic tone in him. What I remember about him most was the constant smirk slowly overtaking his face when someone didn't quite get it. He taught math, and I didn't like that class at all. Math was something I usually excelled in, but I really struggled in his classroom. I hated it when he would ask a question, see that no one was raising his hand, and then raise his eyebrows and whisper loudly, "Murphy!"

Probably my favorite teacher was Mr. Burg for history. He was a big and tough guy, an imposing figure. He was extremely demanding, and it was trouble if you even thought about cutting up in class or not paying attention. Almost every day in class, he would pull a couple of guys out of their seats for fooling around or not being properly prepared and send them to the back wall. There they were forced to stretch their arms out and lean up against the wall, using only their index fingers. After a few minutes, their legs would start to shake and Mr. Burg would go back there and lean on them. It sounds pretty bad now, but it was a different time. He was also one of the most entertaining and organized teachers I've ever known. I enjoyed and learned more in his class than any history course I had ever taken. He just wouldn't tolerate any wise guys.

I didn't mind the discipline at all at Notre Dame. What I did miss were girls and local friends. It just didn't seem natural to take a bunch of young teenage boys and separate them from girls for four years. No matter how good the education was, I felt like I was losing out in social experiences. But the worse part was that it was virtually impossible to get together with the friends you made in high school. The guys I hung around with at school were from West Haven, Milford, Derby, Oxford, Wallingford and New Haven. Also, it took so long to get home each day that I never tried to get involved in any extracurricular activities. In retrospect, I could have found a way, but at that age all I was interested in was getting that long journey home over with at the end of the school day.

City buses would be waiting for us in the afternoon. We would have to push and shove to try to get on one of those buses, often standing when we did. The bus would leave Notre Dame and inch its way through a busy section of West Haven, then move out towards New Haven.

The bus moved slowly up Congress Avenue to get to the downtown area. This was a predominately black section of the city, and there had been riots there the past summer. I found it fascinating, being on that bus, looking out at all the burned-out stores and buildings. People on the street would just stare up at us on the bus in our jackets and ties.

When we got to the downtown area, we had to get the transfer from the bus driver and walk a few blocks to Church and Chapel where we waited by the big Green for the Dixwell Avenue bus. The New Haven Green was a park-like setting with benches, statues, some bums and hundreds of pigeons. There was a great little shop around the corner that sold fresh caramel corn, and we would often stop there for small bags.

Then we would wait a while for the Dixwell to Benham Street bus or the Dixwell to Hamden Plaza bus. Once we were on that, the bus would zigzag its way through the downtown area, go by the Yale buildings and move out toward Lower Dixwell Avenue, the "colored section" I had been through many times with my parents. There weren't as many burned-out buildings here, but I remember staring at all the graffiti on the walls, including lots of "Black Power" slogans. I couldn't wait to get home.

When we finally approached the corner of Dixwell and Wooden Street in Hamden, the buzzer was pulled, and a few of us would pile off the bus. From here, we had a walk of a half mile to our homes. We were always loaded down with tons of books and homework for the night. It was almost 3:45 or 4:00 by the time I got home. Then it was over to Steve Hammond's house to hang around for about an hour until I had to be home for five o'clock supper.

That Halloween, I knew I was getting too old to go out Trick or Treating, but Steve Hammond didn't seem embarrassed by that prospect at all. He talked me into it that afternoon, and together we embarked on what was to be my last night out for Halloween ever. We were too cool to get costumes, but I remember we did find some old clothes and hit the streets. It was OK but it didn't have any of the thrills it had had years earlier, when it was one of the biggest nights of the year for Jimmy Reardon and me.

Back at home, things were a little different in our family. Howie was now away for his first year at Manhattan

College. I was all by myself in our bedroom downstairs, while the rest of the family slept upstairs. That took some getting used to, since I was still remembering Richard Speck and the "Green Man."

Every so often on a Saturday, Mom, Dad, Maureen and I would drive the hour and a half to New York City and visit Howie. College life looked wonderful to me. Howie had lots of friends, and the campus was always alive with activity. We went to a couple of football games, and I had a terrific time cheering for the "Jaspers."

The only thing I didn't like about these visits was the drive to and from the college. There were a few stretches of highway that were too narrow and dangerous. I couldn't get that terrible accident involving the Sacred Heart girls out of my mind. It took a long time for me to stop thinking about that.

It was about this time that a couple of new television shows were becoming popular: *Batman* and *The Monkees*. *Batman* was really popular. People were always talking about how funny that show was, especially with different "guest villains." My favorite was Mr. Freeze.

The best show, however, had to be *The Monkees*. At this point, there was little, if any, regular footage of the Beatles on television. Every once in a great while, they might appear on the *Ed Sullivan Show*, and that would be a big deal, but American kids wanted more. So, when *The Monkees* debuted, it filled the void. Even at my age, I knew that their music couldn't compare with the Beatles, but that didn't matter. All I cared about was that each week, I got to see four mop-heads joking around and playing their music. It worked. I bought their records and played them as religiously as I had the Beatles before. I still think they had some great tunes. My favorites were *A Little Bit Me, A Little Bit You; Look Out Here Comes Tomorrow;* and *You Just May Be The One.* I even tried to find a blue ski cap with a ball on top, just like that of my favorite Monkee, Mike Nesmith.

On Sunday mornings, I was still serving Mass at Saint John the Baptist. That was kind of neat. It was like I was the professional altar boy, returning to the old campus where the younger boys were. A few of us from Notre Dame, who were part of the Saint John's parish, did this, so I got to serve Mass with Tommy Smith and Fred Starno. By this time, things had changed a lot. Mass was now being said in English, as opposed to Latin, and the priest now said Mass on a smaller altar facing the congregation.

Even then, I knew why the changes were made. They wanted the people to be more of a part of the ritual. Everyone could see what the priest was doing, and the prayers were now something everyone could understand. Unfortunately, for me, the mystery and beauty were gone. It had always seemed so holy and magical when the priest was whispering the Consecration prayers in Latin with his back to us. You just had the feeling that a miracle was really taking place. For me it was gone.

Then someone decided it was OK to eat meat on Fridays after all, except for Lent. I really had trouble with this change in Church laws. What about all the people who already had mortal sins for having a hot dog on Friday? What happened to all those souls?

Back at school, Notre Dame had a policy of sending out "unsatisfactory warnings" to parents mid-way through the semester when the student had a D or worse average. These things were known as pink slips. In Howie's four years, he had never received one. One Saturday afternoon in the winter, Mom came into the living room, thumbing through the mail. I remember distinctly how she said, "Here's something from Notre Dame . . . I wonder what this is . . . Oh, my gosh . . . I think it's a PINK SLIP!!!"

You would think I had committed a murder. I never saw Mom and Dad so upset. Naturally, it came from my old nemesis, Brother John Gueriello, the miserable math teacher. He single handedly turned a peaceful Saturday into hysteria.

Over the next few years, the Murphys received enough pink slips that sometimes I didn't even hear about one for a couple of days. I'm convinced they were sent out much more liberally than when Howie went to Notre Dame.

Ironically, the same day we received the pink slip I was supposed to attend my first high school mixer that night. At first, there was no way I was going to be allowed to go, not after causing such disgrace to the family. However, I begged and begged and tried to explain how the other guys who were going with me depended on us to drive them there. Freddy Starno's father was picking us up, but no one could get us there but my father. My parents just had to see how unfair it was to disappoint my friends just because I had failed so miserably. After hours of promising to bring my math grade up, I finally got the OK to go to the mixer.

When I arrived at the mixer that night, I immediately forgot about the crisis of the afternoon. There seemed to be hundreds of Notre Dame students, and girls from everywhere crowded into the gymnasium, listening to the music of N.A.I.F. This was a local band that had actually released a record called "Black on White." N.A.I.F. stood for North Atlantic Invasion Force, and they were rocking the gymnasium from up on the stage. In my eyes, they might as well have been the Beatles.

But the best part had to be the girls. The aroma of cheap perfume filled the gym. For the first time in months, I was near beautiful women. Everywhere I looked, there were girls with long, straight hair just waiting to be asked to dance.

Tommy Smith, Freddy Starno, Gerry Esposito and I stood together, trying to get a feel for the whole thing. We all desperately wanted to be a part of the action but we were all too scared to approach a girl. I thought back to my first dance at the Baltimore Convention and decided the reward of holding a girl in my arms was worth the risk of humiliation if I was turned down for a dance. So I was the first one to leave the safety of the foxhole.

I tried to pick someone who looked to be a Freshman, too, and with trembling legs, asked her if she wanted to dance. Thankfully she said, "yes," and there I was, doing "The Jerk" to the music of N.A.I.F. I ended up asking several different girls to dance that night and maybe I was turned down once or twice but by that time, I was filled with confidence. Naturally, the best part was when a slow dance would start right up after a fast one, and I'd stay on the floor with the girl.

What a great night. I don't think I missed many mixers the rest of my time at Notre Dame. My favorite bands that came to Notre Dame were the Cadavers, Mayflower, Soul Reaction and the Chosen Few.

For four years, while Howie was at Notre Dame, I had attended the annual Spring Festival music show. He had been part of the Glee Club. I loved those shows, so I signed up to be a part of it. Besides the band and singers, there were also a few people who danced on stage. The boys were called the Dancing Knights and the girls were called the Corettes. These were girls from Sacred Heart Academy. I signed up for the Dancing Knights and in January, we began to have practices every Sunday afternoon at the school.

One of the best parts about practice was being picked up in a car each Sunday by a Senior who lived in Hamden, Tommy Downs. This was the first time I went anywhere without a parent driving. You wouldn't believe how cool I felt on a Sunday afternoon at one o'clock when, right in front of the neighborhood kids, Tommy would come pulling up in his father's old black car, and I would climb in with him and go off. I remember the car had a standard shift, and Tommy was just getting the feel for driving it. He really ground the gears a few times, but it didn't matter. I was hanging out with a Senior. Sometimes a few other upper classmen from Hamden would ride with us, too.

The choreographer for the Notre Dame Spring Festival was a fellow named Joe Hayes. He was a real fireball and apparently had a lot of experience in the professional ranks of putting on musicals. I don't know if he got paid or whether his work at Notre Dame was on a voluntary basis, but he was passionate in the way he worked us. Sometimes, he was one of the funniest adults I had ever seen and at other times, he would scream out his disappointment in the way we were rehearsing. All I know is that he was taking a few teenage boys and girls and turning us into a pretty crisp musical act.

By the time Spring Festival came in May, we were pumped up for a great week. The first show was a Sunday matinee performance for the clergy around the state. The gymnasium would be packed with nuns, brothers and priests. I don't think there was any charge for the Sunday show. Then there was a show every night during the week, with the grand finale Saturday night. My family always went to that one.

There was a swing band, singers, dancers and costumes and a pretty slick system of spot lights and special effects. That week was always one of the biggest for me each year. The build-up was great, but the feeling after Saturday night was one of real sadness. In many ways the Spring Festival was similar to Knights of Columbus Conventions. I got all excited with the buildup, thoroughly enjoyed the week-long event and got hit with the letdown when it all ended.

In June of 1967, a war broke out between Israel and her Arab neighbors. Television and newspaper reporters spent a lot of time on it, so I couldn't help but follow it closely. Some of the guys and I would talk about it walking home from the Dixwell Avenue bus stop each afternoon. All I remember is that Israel was "the good guy" and the Arab countries were "the bad guys." It looked like Israel was really kicking their butts pretty good. Everyone seemed surprised that Israel could dominate those countries so easily. The whole thing was over in six days. I couldn't figure out why it was taking the United States so long to do whatever it was that they wanted to do in Vietnam. It seemed like that thing was never ending. It was on TV so much that I was numb to the scenes of helicopters and body bags every night.

While all this went on abroad, at home it was also time for the Notre Dame Freshman picnic at Ocean Beach. Steve Hammond and I spent the day together swimming and going on all the rides. But even though Ocean Beach was twice the size of Lake Quasapaug, it didn't have the same excitement. First of all, there were no girls with us. Second of all, I think the thrill of amusement parks was starting to diminish a little bit as I got older. Granted, it was still better than sitting in class but it wasn't such a big deal.

That summer, I went to a pool party one night at a girl's house in Hamden. Rosanne Milano had gone to Saint John the Baptist with me, and she invited a bunch of people over. I was pretty excited about going to my first official boy-girl party but when I got there, I only knew a few people. I had been asked to bring some records so, naturally, I brought some Beatles and Monkees' albums. I couldn't believe that people were not into those groups like I was. I remember listening to the Beach Boys and the Young Rascals most of the night. I felt a little lost at that party, but things turned out pretty good later because we had a big scavenger hunt and then played spin the bottle. The best looking girls were already with their boyfriends, and they didn't play. It wasn't great, but it was OK.

At that time, I was also spending more time with Fred Starno and Chuck Page. Chuck was a close friend of Fred's, but the three of us started to hang around together quite a bit. I started to do lots of things with their families, including Sunday dinners and bigger events. Mr. Starno enjoyed taking us to small stadiums around the state to watch big marching bands compete. We also went to a few baseball games in New York City.

One time, we all went down to Shea Stadium with Chuck's family to see the Mets play. Chuck's grandfather was a big Mets fan, and it was my first trip to see them play. The best part of that day was before the game started. It was announced that Hollywood was filming there for a scene in an upcoming movie called *The Odd Couple*. They were going to film a triple play by the Mets, and all of us in the stadium were going to be part of the movie. It took several takes to get it right, but they finally pulled it off. That was pretty cool.

During the summers, while you were a Notre Dame student, you had to read five books. Once you got back to school in September, you had a big exam waiting for you in English class. It wasn't bad enough that you had that hanging over your head all summer, but the books they had us read were the worst books imaginable. We had to read things like *Moby Dick, The Oxbow Incident, Watch For a Tall White Sail, The Pearl* and *Great Expectations*. It was almost impossible for me to sit down and read that junk. Why in God's name couldn't they give fourteen-year-old boys some books that would keep our interest? I loved to read and would have been perfectly happy to read five books, but it was torture trying to get through those five. These were classics? It made no sense.

That August was the annual convention for the Knights of Columbus. This time, we were leaving the country and driving up to Montreal, Canada. The best part of this convention was that there was a World's Fair going on there called Expo '67. Besides the usual activities they had planned for the teenagers, my friends and I could take a train from under the hotel right out to Expo '67 and spend the day there. It was fabulous! Tommy Dechant, Jim Griffin, Joey from Canada and I went out there almost every day. We went through every exhibition and also spent a lot of time at the amusement park.

Tommy, Jimmy and I had our own room at this convention, so we could come and go as we pleased as long as we behaved ourselves. We stayed at a beautiful place called the Queen Elizabeth Hotel in downtown Montreal. Right across the street was a big cathedral and one day, a bishop who was a good friend of the Griffin family asked us to serve Mass for him there. That was quite a thrill. The bishop was as down-to-earth as anyone you could meet. We really liked him.

One of the best parts about Montreal was the way the hotel sat above levels of activity. Below the lobby, underground, was a big shopping plaza. Below that there were subways and trains. It was like a different city once you went below the surface. I was also fascinated with how everyone in Montreal said everything twice, once in English and once in French. Even the elevator operator would say, "Up please" and then say the same thing in French. The waitress would greet you in English and then again in French. Finally, I really liked that you could exchange an American dollar for more than a dollar in Canadian money.

When the convention started to die down and people were saying good-bye, we were already looking forward to 1968. We were all going to Disneyland, California. That would turn out to be something special.

Right near the very end of summer, Fred and I were over at Chuck's house on Circular Avenue. As usual, there were lots of his relatives around. That evening, I met a couple of his girl cousins who came by. One was Susan Griffiths. I couldn't keep my eyes off of her all night. I remember us being outside in the warm air and I just stole glances for hours. I don't think we spoke to each other once, but she certainly had a huge impact on me. That girl would be on my mind every day for almost a whole year.

Chapter Eleven

1967–1968

Assassinations, Hippies and A Kiss

At almost fifteen years old, I was back to Notre Dame High School. After a Freshman year of Cs and Bs, I started my second year more determined to be on top of my studies. Actually, I felt this optimism at the start of every school year. I think it was the smell of the new books and fresh, clean notebooks. There were no scribble marks, doodles or large initials all over the material. I just knew that as long as I kept things neat and organized, I would get As and Bs. This feeling usually lasted about a week.

It was fun being a Sophomore now. The Freshmen at school those first few days looked so young and lost at the big high school. Later that week, the first pep rally of the year didn't disappoint me. Tradition called for us to boo and laugh at the new students, and we made a lot of noise.

I think the Sophomores were the most vocal, probably because it was the first time we weren't in that lowly position.

I was now spending most of my after-school and weekend time with Fred Starno and Chuck Page. Chuck's cousins lived a couple of streets over from Fred in the Saint John's neighborhood. We started to see more of them that fall.

Naturally, I was falling head over heels for Susan Griffiths. She was just too pretty. But, she was very quiet and that made it even more difficult for me to talk to her. I mostly fumbled around when she was near me.

The first Notre Dame mixer that fall was scheduled for a Friday night, and Chuck and Fred told me that Susan was going to be there. I was part thrilled and part ready to throw up because I didn't know if I had the guts to ask her to dance.

I got to the mixer and sure enough, there was Susan. No girl ever looked better. Her hair was getting longer, and she was a vision in that gymnasium that night. She was standing with a group of girls, and I was trying to summon up enough courage to go up to her and ask her for a dance. So many times, I started to walk over but I just couldn't move my feet.

Finally, a couple of other guys, Juniors, went over to the group and stood there talking for a couple of minutes. I just about died when I saw Susan go off for a fast dance with one of them. This was the jolt I needed to get me going. If I didn't make my move soon, I'd lose her for life.

I waited for that dance to end then dove right into the situation. Shaking like a leaf, I walked up to her and asked, "Would you like to dance?" She mumbled OK, and we danced a fast dance, not saying a word to each other. I would occasionally glance at her and watch her move to the music. She was taking my breath away.

When it ended, the band moved right into a slow number and before I could think about it too much, I asked her if she would like to dance again. She said, "OK" and slipped into my arms.

I suppose there are greater feelings people have experienced, but that was and still is one of the greatest feelings I have ever had in my entire life. It just felt so right.

I remember vividly how sometimes I would actually fall off the beat a little bit, hanging on my left side when I was supposed to move to my right. That way I could feel her slide across me for a split second. Hey, I wasn't even fifteen years old yet. It was a great move.

The dance finally ended, and I asked her if she would like a Coke. Again she said, "OK" and we went off to the table where they sell the sodas. We stood there drinking the Cokes, and I couldn't think of a thing to say. A group of our friends came by, and eventually we went our separate ways. I danced with Susan a couple of more times that night. I thought it was just a matter of time before she and I were to be boyfriend and girlfriend.

It's funny how big things can happen about the same time. That weekend, Bonnie Lipton and her family were moving away from Furman Road and over to the Westville Section of New Haven. Although most of my thoughts were about Susan, I was pretty sad saying good-bye to Bonnie. She had been "my girl" for most of my life. We had played baseball, football and basketball together our whole lives. We had swung on vines down the woods. Now that she was turning into a beautiful young woman, she was leaving.

Fred and Chuck were really into bowling and were part of a Saturday afternoon league at the Hamden Lanes at the Hamden Mart. I joined their team and was part of the league for my entire Sophomore year. Susan and her cousin also bowled in the league, too. I got to see her every Saturday. We never spoke to each other.

Why was it so hard? Didn't she remember the dance we had a few weeks earlier? Wasn't she feeling what I was feeling? It was like nothing had ever happened.

That October, Dad got a big promotion with the Knights of Columbus. He was now called the Assistant Supreme Secretary. Though my parents never talked about money with us, I had the feeling that his salary was much larger. Always fairly conservative in their spending and lifestyle, my parents were now looking for a big color television set.

My family was also making plans to spend a long weekend in New York City that winter. On top of that, Dad said we could all go with him to the State Deputy's meeting the following June which was going to be in Williamsburg, Virginia. This was a sort of mini-convention. I was thrilled with that news. Now I was going to get to go on more Knights of Columbus trips each year. The big Supreme Convention for the following summer was to be in Disneyland, California. I don't think we had really expected to go because it was so expensive, but now Dad said we could all look forward to flying to California.

The only drawback to all this good news was that Mom and Dad were now starting to talk about possibly moving to a larger home. I didn't like the idea of leaving Furman Road at all. I remember being worried about that for several days but gradually, that kind of talk faded away. It would be a few years later, while I was in college, when we finally moved.

I started watching a show called *Hogan's Heroes* that fall and I thought it was just about the best thing on television

I had seen in a long time. I loved the drum roll that started each show. My father really loved this show, too. I can still remember him howling when Sergeant Shultz made one of his shocked faces upon running into the prisoners in town or maybe in Paris.

One Saturday night, I went to the movies with Chuck, Fred and another cousin of Chuck's, Kathy. We went downtown in New Haven to the Roger Sherman Theater where we saw the thriller, *Wait Until Dark.*

It was a story about a blind woman, Audrey Hepburn, who somehow became the victim of some drug dealers. A killer entered her apartment at the end of the movie, and she had to fight for her life, breaking all the lights and light bulbs in her home so the killer couldn't see, either. This was one of the most intense movies I had ever seen. It just about scared me to death. For many nights afterwards, I couldn't get to sleep, still seeing that man, slipping on the plastic gloves before trying to murder Audrey. I was now fifteen years old but was wishing that Howie wasn't away at college, leaving me to sleep by myself.

We started playing tackle football every Saturday morning over at Eli Whitney High School. A lot of guys from Chuck's neighborhood joined us for big games. Most of us had some equipment to wear. A lot of guys wore shoulder pads only, but I felt a lot better wearing a helmet. I used to fantasize about Susan Griffiths coming to these Saturday morning games and, of course, watching me make some sort of brave tackle or great play. She would have been so impressed!

That winter, I remember being over at Chuck's house for lunch on Saturday. It was a three family house and the boy who lived downstairs from him had a new Beatles album. We all went down to look at it and listen to the songs. It was called *Sergeant Peppers Lonely Hearts Club Band* but it didn't look like the Beatles. It didn't sound like the Beatles. I had no idea what the music was all about. The guys said that this was an album they had made while they were on LSD.

I didn't like this change at all. These people were not the Beatles I had loved so much. It was scary to think that they could all go off the deep end so quickly.

Back at Notre Dame, things were going pretty well. My favorite day of the week was Wednesday when I didn't have to bring my lunch. This was the day that the cafeteria sold meatball subs, and I could have that. Most of the students and teachers always joked about how bad they were. They called the meatballs "golf balls in brown soup," but I thought they were fantastic. I would rush from class at lunch time to be one of the first in line.

Instead of taking a study hall as most students did, I signed up for an elective that year, typing. My parents and Howie had told me that learning to type at a young age would be one of the best things I could do. They turned out to be right.

I loved typing class with Brother Francis. He would drape a large cloth from the typewriter up to your chin, with your hands underneath it on the keyboard, to prevent us from looking at our fingers and keys. I quickly became proficient at typing, probably because I practiced so much in my mind during every waking hour. I was constantly moving my fingers, typing out words on an imaginary typewriter. Usually, I was typing out something to do with Susan Griffiths.

That holiday season was big for NFL football. I really got caught up in the play-offs. I enjoyed watching Roman Gabriel of the Los Angeles Rams and Bart Starr of the Green Bay Packers quarterback their teams. The networks now had something called "instant replay" where you could watch the big plays over and over again.

The biggest game that season was the NFL championship between the Dallas Cowboys and Green Bay. The so-called "Super Bowl" was still thought of as more or less an exhibition game following the season, so the game they played on December thirty-first was really for all the marbles.

They played up in Green Bay, and I think the temperature was minus twelve degrees. The stadium was packed, and all you could see was steam coming out of the fans and players as they breathed. I couldn't imagine what it was like slamming into people or the ground when it was that cold. However, they played that football game right down to the wire. Bart Starr led the Packers down the field in the closing minutes, behind by three points. With just a few seconds left in the game, he took the ball himself for a quarterback sneak following Jerry Kramer's block, squirming his way into the end zone for the victory. It was one of the greatest football games I had ever seen. Years later it was referred to as the "Ice Bowl."

In February of 1968, as promised, my parents took Maureen and me to New York City for a long weekend. We met up with Howie for dinner, but he had to go back to campus later that night. I remember it was bitter cold, but we had a terrific time those few days. We saw Rockefeller Center and the filming of a game show and ate in some great restaurants.

On our last day in New York, we got to go to Radio City Music Hall where we saw the Rockettes dance. Then we saw a movie. It was called *Sweet November.* It was the story of a young woman who apparently was dying of some mysterious disease. She would take a lover each month, trying to get in a lifetime of romance and adventure in the little time she had left. The problem was, the man who was with her for the month of November fell deeply in love with her, and she had strong feelings for him, too.

This was the first movie I had ever seen that didn't have your typical happy ending. He wanted to stay with her but finally backed off when he knew the full story. The movie ended with him watching from a distance as she met her man for the month of December, a nerdy type of guy who probably needed her more than she needed him.

Driving home to Connecticut, I couldn't stop thinking about that woman. She stayed on my mind for a couple of weeks.

We were still going to church every Sunday morning at Saint John's, and I was still an altar boy. I was probably one of the oldest ones there, but it was the only chance I had to get close to Susan Griffiths every week. I made sure I always got the "book side" as opposed to the "bells side" so I would be in the right place at Communion time.

When the congregation members made their way up to the altar to get their hosts, I would accompany the priest with my "host catcher," the little plate held under the person's chin in case the host fell. My hand always shook a little when I looked into Susan's face, her eyes closed as she opened her mouth to receive communion. It was all I could do not to bend down and kiss her.

I was spending most of my time now with Chuck and Fred. The bicycle I received for my tenth birthday was never put to more use than it was my Sophomore year. Both Chuck and Fred lived about a mile from me, and we were constantly going back and forth from one house to another.

I felt like I was part of their families. Chuck's parents were good to all of us, and I really enjoyed going over to Fred's, too. There I had some of the best Italian dinners I ever tasted. In my house about the only Italian food we had was out of the can. Over at Fred's house, I was treated to fabulous Italian cooking.

I was beginning to learn more about things that were happening in the world. I had an English teacher during Sophomore year, Mr. Christiansen. He was probably the best teacher I've ever had in my life. He was a very quiet and gentle man with a trim beard, which was rather unusual for Notre Dame. That spring, he not only taught English class but would often discuss social and political events which were taking place. We learned a lot about the war going on in Vietnam. Something had happened there in January, the Tet Offensive. For the first time it didn't look certain that the United States was going to win a war. It didn't make much sense to me.

Mr. Christiansen was also into pop music. Sometimes, he would bring in a small record player and play us songs, handing out the lyrics on photocopies. We studied things like *Ruby Tuesday* from the Rolling Stones, *I Am A Rock* from Simon and Garfunkel, and *Eleanor Rigby* from the Beatles. He encouraged us to grab every moment in life, to pursue our dreams and try not to be afraid.

Mr. Christiansen's class was late in the day and by that time, I was just lazy enough to thoroughly enjoy his discussions. He had a hypnotizing effect on me. It was probably the only class I ever had where I wanted time to stop. I hated it when the bell rang at the end.

Howie came home one weekend, and I remember my parents talking to him about his bad knee. I guess he had something wrong with it and had gone to a couple of doctors. Mom and Dad thought that Howie had a chance to avoid being drafted if he had a bad knee. I guess Vietnam was starting to make them a little nervous, too.

One night in the spring of '68 I was over at Steve Hammond's house. His father told us to quiet down as a big news bulletin was coming on television. We gathered round and watched. President Johnson was speaking to the nation, announcing that he was not going to run for a second term. Steve's parents said it was because of the problems in Vietnam. Again . . . Vietnam. More and more, you heard about Vietnam. You heard it in school, at home and saw it every night on TV. Now it was making the United States President not want to be President anymore.

That same season, there was another special bulletin coming across television. It was announced that Martin Luther King had been assassinated down in Memphis, Tennessee. I had heard of him, of course, but I was under the impression he was dangerous. I knew about Malcom X, and the name alone sounded scary to me as a White person. I guess I just assumed Martin Luther King didn't like White people. I didn't feel good or bad when I learned he was killed.

Over the next few days, I learned a lot more about him. He wasn't scary at all. The networks were revealing his life's accomplishments and what he had been trying to do for the country. I found myself glued to the television the same way I was back in 1963 when President Kennedy was killed. I was especially mesmerized when I saw his body on a little wagon, too, with mules instead of horses pulling it.

I also remember seeing Senator Robert Kennedy give a little speech to many Black people when they found out about King's death. He spoke of him like America was going to be a lot worse off now that he was gone.

Just as we were winding down the school year, yet another special bulletin came across our television. It always started the same way, "We interrupt this program to bring you a special bulletin from CBS News." I was starting to hate them. This time another shooting had taken place. Robert Kennedy had been gunned down at a hotel after winning the California primary. Over and over again, we saw the television footage of the chaos after the shooting, including close-ups of Kennedy lying on the ground, his head in a pool of blood.

You would think that I would be numb to all the events that were taking place, but this one bothered me a lot. I was still a big fan of the Kennedy mystique and assumed that Robert Kennedy was going to be elected President the following November. I figured he was going to straighten out all the problems I had been hearing about.

The doctors operated on him, and I expected him to survive. The newspaper and TV all showed diagrams of just how the bullet entered his head and what damage there was. He only lasted about a day before he died.

Just like I had years earlier, I followed everything very closely. I was older now and understood much more than I did when President John Kennedy was killed. There was a train that went through many big cities, carrying Robert Kennedy's body to the funeral. Thousands of people waited at every stop. Sometimes, we would get a glimpse of his wife, Ethel. It brought back all the bad memories of November 1963.

At the funeral, Ted Kennedy gave the eulogy. I'll never forget how he stood up in that cathedral, his voice shaking as he spoke of his brother. I can still recite it word for word.

A couple of weeks later, it was the last day of school. On the way home, I went to a record store downtown and picked up four records, all 45s: *Jumping Jack Flash* by the Rolling Stones; *Hello, I Love You* by The Doors; *I Love You* by The People; and *Sunshine of Your Love* by Cream. These were the first records I had bought in years that were not by the Beatles or the Monkees. I guess I was still protesting the dramatic change in the Beatles' appearance and music.

Later in June, the family went on the "mini-convention," the State Deputies' meeting in Williamsburg, Virginia. This convention didn't have all the scheduled events that the big convention had every August, but we were in a wonderful place to tour. Tom Dechant, Jim Griffin and I naturally spent all our time together. We had our own room again and had a fantastic time.

On our last night there, poor Jim got into a lot of trouble by going off on his own for awhile. All of the mothers there were pretty upset when we didn't know where he was. A few of us went out with our fathers looking for him, and we finally found Jim a couple of hours later. His father was pretty mad at him when we got back to the hotel.

On the way back home to Connecticut, we stopped in Gettysburg, Pennsylvania to see the battlefield. What I thought was going to be a boring couple of days turned out to be unbelievable. I saw and walked on Seminary Ridge, Cemetery Ridge, Cemetery Hill, Big Round Top, Little Round Top and The Angle. One of my favorite parts of the visit was "The Electric Map." Here, a small audience sat in a room looking down in the dark at a great big map. There were hundreds of tiny light bulbs that went on and off showing the movement of the Union and Confederate Armies. It was fascinating.

When I got home, I looked up the name of every Civil War officer who I remembered being in the Battle of Gettysburg. That trip stirred a fever in me for the Civil War that would continue into adulthood.

I guess it was the year of trips. Usually, Dad had to work on all our vacations, so he wanted to take a week off and go somewhere he didn't have to work. It had been several years since we had been to Cape Cod so it was decided we would go up there again.

Howie, of course, was too old to want to go on vacation with his family, but Grandma Vivian went along with us. We did all the usual things we had done years before: the miniature golf, the penny candy store and even some of the regular restaurants. But while it was fun, it wasn't the same. It just seemed like a different place than where I had been when I was younger. There was a letdown because those great feelings I had in Cape Cod as a little boy weren't there when I was fifteen.

During the summer, all we did was talk about our big trip out to California in August. I was going to be flying for the first time, too. We were going on American Airlines. I was going to see Disneyland and the Pacific Ocean, and we were even going to drive up to San Francisco at the end of the convention. This was going to be some kind of a trip.

August finally came, and we were off to Kennedy Airport in New York City for the flight. Even Howie was coming along for this vacation. I got a window seat on the right side of the plane. I will never forget the thrill of racing down that runway, faster and faster, finally leaving the ground and going up into the sky. The view was tremendous. We were in that plane for hours, but I never got bored. First of all, I found that I loved eating on an airplane. People made fun of airplane food, but I thought it was great. (Still do!) We had a big dinner and then we got to see a movie, *The Odd Couple.* It was the same movie for which I saw the filming of the triple play at Shea Stadium. I loved it!

I was able to look down at the Mississippi River and the Rocky Mountains. When we approached Los Angeles, I remember the plane slowing down and turning to the left. It felt like we were stopping in mid-air. It was a strange sensation. The landing was even more exciting than the take-off. Even though we had been slowing down for a few minutes, you really got an idea of how fast you were going because you were so much closer to the ground. I loved everything about my first airplane flight.

Out in California, I saw the official "hippies" I had seen on television for the last year or so. I remember the guys were rather nasty looking, but the girls were beautiful, especially the ones with flowers in their hair. The other thing I noticed out there was that everyone was talking about the newest singing sensation, Tiny Tim. That I couldn't figure out at all. Was this what people thought was good entertainment? If Tiny Tim was popular, what was going to be next? I guess I took things a little too seriously. I don't know why I couldn't do what everyone else was doing, laugh and enjoy the big excitement for a couple of months.

The convention started a few days later. Most of the day activities naturally centered on Disneyland itself, but there were other things to enjoy as well. One day, all the teen-agers went off on a bus to a beach. While waiting to go, I kept noticing a pretty young girl with long dark hair and bangs, wearing a floppy straw hat. She had a great tan which really showed off her pearl white teeth. I don't know why I remember her teeth so vividly.

She was with a group of friends, but somehow we struck up a conversation, and she was as bubbly and friendly as any girl I had ever met. Her name was Rosemary May, and she was from Crown Point, Indiana. I kept my eye on her on the bus ride out to the beach. I finally got a chance to swim in the Pacific Ocean that day. The waves were so much bigger than I had seen on Long Island Sound or even up on Cape Cod. I found Rosemary body surfing with her friends so I hung around her trying to get to know her better. Every once in a while, a great big wave would come along and knock us all over the place. She went underwater a couple of times, and I found myself grabbing her hand to help her up. I kept hoping for more big waves so I could hold her hand more and I wasn't disappointed.

We spent the whole day together. Late in the afternoon when I was on the bus, I saw her and her friends coming down the aisle. The seat next to me was vacant and I slid over, hoping she would sit down with me. When she did, I was afraid I would freeze up. But Rosemary was very easy to talk to, and everything was perfect.

I remember how she was sitting on my left and I wanted so badly to reach over and hold her hand, but I couldn't do it. My left hand was down by my leg and she must have sensed what I wanted to do, because her right hand kept dropping down closer and closer to mine until it finally fell into my hand. As our hands squeezed, I couldn't help but think how the feeling was just as intense as when I had that slow dance with Susan Griffiths at that September mixer. I was in heaven.

The rest of the trip was just too good to be true. Rosemary and I spent our days at Disneyland and nights at different social events planned for the convention teenagers. On the last night of the convention, there was a big dance, and I met Rosemary there. She was breathtaking in her blue dress, and we spent the whole night dancing with each other like there was no one else around. It was over at 11:00 p.m., and I walked her to her hotel which was on the other side of the park. It was a little awkward saying goodnight. I had had a little kissing experience from the spin the bottle parties, but this kiss was longer and sweeter than anything I had ever known.

With my head still floating and my brain turned to mush, I somehow had to find my way back to the Disneyland Hotel. I remember my brother meeting me a couple of blocks away, telling me that I was in big trouble for getting home so late. It wasn't nearly as big a deal as when Jimmy Griffin was missing in Williamsburg, but I caught hell from Mom and Dad. Still, it couldn't put a damper on what I was feeling that night.

The next day, the convention was over, and my family and I headed up to San Francisco in a rental car for a few days. I just stared out the window of the back seat thinking about every minute I had spent with Rosemary. I suppose I should have been happy after the wonderful week I had had, but I was overwhelmed with sadness. I missed her so much and wondered if I would ever see her again.

I did remember to ask my father to stop the car near the ocean since I had promised Fred Starno that I would get him some Pacific Ocean water in an old peanut butter jar. I did that and sealed it up for the return trip.

Up in San Francisco, my family really seemed to enjoy the sights, but I was in a daze. I went through the motions but hardly remembered anything about that part of our vacation. I don't remember much about the plane ride home, either. I guess I was finally over Susan Griffiths.

Chapter Twelve

1968–1969

Letters from Rosemary, Driving and Apollo 11

I went back to Notre Dame High School for my Junior year. With all the things that had happened in the world in 1968, I wasn't surprised when Mr. Antonetti, our homeroom teacher, told us that we were living through critical times. 1968 had already seen assassinations, war, racial issues, riots at the Democratic Convention in Chicago and more and more drug use. I remember him talking to us about the Olympic athletes who raised their fists in the Black Power salute while they were accepting their medals. He wanted to know what we thought about that protest. I didn't have any feelings about it one way or another. Thinking about all that kind of stuff sometimes got too crazy. Besides, all I could think about was one thing: recreating every day I had spent in Disneyland with Rosemary May, especially trying to remember every second of that kiss.

I couldn't believe how stupid I was for not getting her address on the trip. Getting it now took weeks of my writing to Joey in Canada, and him writing to a girl he had met at the convention who knew Rosemary's address. Finally, I got her address and that night, I wrote her a letter. Within a few days, I got one from her.

A letter usually took two or three days to get to her. Once five days had elapsed, I would rush home to see if I had one waiting in return. Sometimes, the mailman would come late in the afternoon, and I would almost knock him over trying to see if there was a familiar envelope.

Rosemary was two years younger than me and was just beginning her first year in high school. But she was going off to an all-girls boarding school in Lake Forest, Illinois.

We told each other everything that we were doing. We wrote about school, our friends and music. I remember how she told me about hearing the song *Abraham, Martin and John* for the first time and how it made her cry. This was a song about all good men who had been assassinated.

I thought about her all the time, wondering what she was doing each minute. It took a little while to get used to the fact that she was in a different time zone. Whatever she was doing, it was an hour earlier there. She signed her first couple of letters "Luv, Rosemary." Then for a while, it was "Love Ya, Rosemary" and finally, "Love, Rosemary." I don't know why, but that was important to me.

Fred Starno started to write to one of Rosemary's friends at Lake Forest. I think her name was Becky. They had never met, of course, but were pen pals for a year or so.

Back in the real world, the presidential elections were coming up, Nixon against Humphrey. I happened to see a half-hour special advertisement for Nixon one night while I was down in the basement. I was very much impressed with what he had to say. He just seemed to have all the answers to all our problems. I suppose if I saw a half-hour advertisement for Humphrey, I would have felt the same way about him. In any event, I found myself rooting for Nixon in the November election.

The skyline in New Haven was changing. The Knights of Columbus Supreme Headquarters was building a new twenty-two story tower. It would not be ready for a while, but it was great watching it go up. I was able to get a good look at the downtown area from the windows of my afternoon classes during my Junior year. It was pretty cool to think I knew so many of the men who would be in that building. It also made me think of the last Knights of Columbus Convention and Rosemary May. Underneath my jacket and tie, I always wore a little string of "love beads" that Rosemary had made for me in Disneyland. No one ever knew I had them on.

I started watching a television show that fall because everyone was talking about it, *Laugh-In*. It was a one-hour comedy that was supposed to be so hip, so modern that all cool people were supposed to love it. I tried and tried to get into it but I just thought it was dull. It was one of those things where I had to sit through about 55 minutes of stupid jokes to get a decent laugh here and there. The only thing I really liked about *Laugh-In* was watching Goldie Hawn. She was a doll.

That football season, all the local media personalities could talk about was Joe Namath of the New York Jets. My New York Giants were a pretty bad team in the late sixties, and all the hype was about the Jets, who were in the playoffs in the AFL. The team advanced to the World

Championship game against the NFL champion Baltimore Colts. I think it was right about this time or maybe right after the game that people started referring to this game every January as the Super Bowl.

That Sunday, Howie and a lot of his friends were over at our house watching the big game with Dad and me. All of us were rooting for the traditional NFL team, the Baltimore Colts, except for Paul Keating. He was all by himself cheering on the New York Jets. As the game progressed, even the television announcers started to get caught up in the excitement of the Jets looking like they were going to upset the Colts. Suddenly, the AFL was for real. It was just a matter of time before the two leagues combined into one. Joe Namath and the Jets won that game, but the real fun for me was being part of that big crowd at my house. It was as good as being at the stadium.

That winter, I started listening to the old Sergeant Peppers album. Jimmy Griffin and all his brothers must have had an extra copy of it, so Jimmy had given me one. I found myself liking it more and more, playing it in my room when I was trying to do my homework. Then I picked up the *Magical Mystery Tour* album and listened to that just as much. I was getting back into the Beatles again. They were still better than anything else I was hearing on the radio. I went back and started listening to some of their "middle" albums again like *Rubber Soul, Revolver* and *Yesterday and Today*.

Now that I was 16, it was time to get a Social Security Number as well as my working papers. I put in an application at Soybel's Drug Store at the corner of Dixwell Avenue and Woodin Street. My brother and some of his friends had worked there, so it was the natural place for me to apply for a part-time job. Most of my friends were applying for jobs, too, mainly at grocery stores.

It was about this time that I started going to drivers' education class at Notre Dame every Saturday morning. We saw films of horrible accidents that were supposed to scare us. I did not need those films. I still remembered those three girls from Sacred Heart who died years earlier.

I was also starting to practice driving when I was home. For some reason, I thought it would be helpful to go back and forth, up and down my driveway. Driving around Hamden with my mother or father was pretty easy, since I was going forward all the time.

Eventually, it was time for the big driving test to get a license. About forty of us were at school during a vacation week, all taking our written tests and eye examinations. Once everybody passed, we had to go out and drive with a man from the Department of Motor Vehicles.

There was a lot of talk about how the guy who was testing you might try to pull a trick on you to see if you were alert to all the rules. We heard he might tell you to turn into a one way street going the wrong way or tell you to drive a little faster than the speed limit. Naturally, we were not going to fall for anything like that. We were also told by our driving teacher how important it was for you and the examiner to have your seat belts on.

As luck would have it, I was called up first to go with the man. He was dressed in uniform and looked like one of those old fat guys you see from a movie, a southern-type sheriff with sunglasses on. He was pretty matter-of-fact when he got into the passenger side of the car and told me to pull away from the parking lot.

I put my seat belt on and asked him to please put his on as well. He said, "That's OK, son, we are just going a little ways." I kind of smiled to myself, knowing that he was trying to trick me into driving while a passenger was not wearing his seat belt. I calmly replied, "I'm sorry sir, but all passengers need to wear their seat belts while I am driving."

I half expected him to congratulate me on knowing the rules, but he looked a little bit annoyed and repeated, "I said we are just going a little ways, so let's get going." I smiled again and thought, "Boy, this guy is pretty good!" Again, I said to him, "I am very sorry, sir, but you need to put your seat belt on before I can drive the car."

This time, he jumped out of the car and shouted, "That was your last chance!" He stormed off into the building to get another student, leaving me in the car. I thought to myself, "Boy, this guy is really good, he'll be back any second!"

He did come back, but with another student. He ordered me out of the car and took off with the other candidate. I walked into the classroom and tried to answer all the questions the other guys were asking me. Our driving teacher said he would talk to the examiner when he got back, but I figured that I was finished.

I guess the examiner heard the story from my teacher and gave me another chance but I was the last one to take my drive. I passed easily but could not help thinking how much I wanted to slam on the brakes and watch that fat jerk crash into the windshield. However, I behaved myself and got my license.

That spring, I started working at Soybel's drug store. Ernie Soybel was the boss and pharmacist. He had an elderly father named Abe who sometimes came in to help out. Bob and Fred, who were pharmacists, also worked there. Most of the clerks were high school and college students who worked there part-time.

On my first day, I was pretty nervous. There seemed to be a million things to learn. I found something out about myself while trying to learn that job. I was pretty thick when it came to learning new things, but once I learned something, I remembered it forever. I would be this way for the rest of my life.

I learned how to make change at the cash register, stock shelves, sell cigars, process utility bills and do inventory. I still remember that the cost for cigarettes was 33¢ in the spring of 1969. Out of $1.00, you gave back two, one, one, two . . . two pennies, one nickel, one dime, and two quarters. Gary Poole taught me that one.

My schedule was Monday, Wednesday, and Friday from 6:00–9:00 p.m. one week and Tuesday from 6:00–9:00 p.m. and Saturday afternoons from 1:00–6:00 p.m. the other week. I know these were not a lot of work hours, but they always seemed to screw up any of the plans I wanted to make. I guess I, once again, just did not want any responsibility. When I got to the store, it was not bad at all but I never had that great weekend feeling on Friday afternoon when I knew I had to work the next day. Maybe I was just lazy.

I got to work with some really nice people at Soybel's. One girl that I especially remember was Linda Onofrio. She was considered to be one of the prettiest girls at Hamden High School but she was also very nice. She was always having trouble with her boyfriend.

That spring, I started to spend more time with my old pal from St. John's, Tom Smith. He and I were now in most of each other's classes. He went to a mixer at Notre Dame with Fred and me. He knew several of the girls at Sacred Heart and always seemed to have an on-again, off-again romance with a girl named Paula. I met a girl in this Sacred Heart crowd named Lena Bolduc. We danced several times that night and had a nice time together.

The next week, Notre Dame had a Wednesday off for a teacher's workshop. Smitty and I decided to go over to

Hamden Duck Pin Bowling Lanes because Smitty learned that a class of Sophomores from Sacred Heart was bowling as part of its gym requirements.

We tried to stay in the background because all the girls were being chaperoned by a handful of nuns. This was not the place to work on our social skills. But I did keep watching Lena and once in the while, she'd look over at me. I kept smiling and giving a subtle wave, but she kept looking a little bit shy and confused. I just assumed she was a little nervous with all the nuns around so I kept it up. I noticed she kept whispering things to her friends, and they'd all look over at me, so I kept smiling and waving. Finally after a few minutes of this, Smitty asked why I was waving to that girl. I said, "Why not?" He said that I didn't even know her. It was a girl named Adrienne.

It turned out that Lena was way down at the other end of the alleys, and I was smiling and waving to a girl who looked a little bit like her. I guess it had been pretty dark at that mixer. Naturally, Smitty was in stitches, and the word got around quickly of my mistake. That was a little embarrassing.

I was still very much involved in the Dancing Knights, practicing every Sunday and getting ready for the Spring Festival in May. I found myself very interested in a pretty girl who had long, shiny dark hair. She was in several of the numbers with me and seemed very friendly, but I only talked to her a couple of times. Her name was Debbi Merkel.

There was another Friday night mixer at Notre Dame, and I noticed her there, standing around with a group of friends from Sacred Heart. I spent a few minutes mustering up enough courage to ask her for a dance and she accepted.

After two or three fast dances, I asked her if she wanted to get a Coke, and she agreed. We stood and talked for a little while. When the band played a slow tune, I asked her if she'd like to dance again. I was lucky enough for the band to play *Hey Jude*, which is a very long song. By the end of that slow dance, I wasn't missing Rosemary May as much.

Debbi was from a town a few miles from where I lived, Wallingford. One of her good friends, Peggy Sands, started spending time with Fred Starno, so we met them at school mixers for the next few weeks.

Sundays were even more special now. In our practices for the Spring Festival, sometimes Debbi and I would sit in the bleachers waiting for our dance numbers. We would hold hands and talk. I felt like a million bucks when I was with her.

Working at Soybel's was beginning to be a nuisance as far as seeing Debbi was concerned. The actual job itself was OK, but it was interfering with my love life.

During homeroom in the morning, the announcements would come over the PA system concerning different upcoming events, and I would always be on the edge of my seat waiting to hear if the next mixer was on a Friday night or on a Saturday night. When it was announced that a mixer was scheduled for a Friday night, it always seemed to be on the week where I had to work from 6:00 p.m. to 9:00 p.m. That meant I couldn't see Debbi.

On Holy Thursday, Notre Dame had a half day, so Fred and I met Debbi and Peggy in downtown New Haven. The four of us had lunch and spent the afternoon walking around the New Haven Green. Debbi and I had a bag of popcorn and fed the pigeons. At about 4:30, we had to go our separate ways and catch buses back to our homes.

When I entered my house that evening, another pink slip was waiting for me on the kitchen counter. It was hardly mentioned at the dinner table. My father said something about it "being time for me to buckle down."

Spring Festival was the best ever in 1969. Not only was there the usual anticipation and excitement for putting on the show, I was going to be with Debbi every night for a week.

It was such a great few days. Sometimes when Debbi was in one of her numbers and I had some free time, I would climb up the ladders on the side of the stage to go into the spotlight booths. A friend of mine, Andy Nemit, worked on the lights, and I would sit up there with him for a little while, helping him shine the spotlight on the singers and dancers. I kind of envied him sitting up there. He didn't have to be on stage, yet he was a big part of the show behind the scenes.

On Saturday night, we had the Grand Finale. My family was there and after the show, I brought Debbi out into the audience and introduced her to them. I remember Debbi being very nervous about meeting my mother and father. Later, there was a party in the cafeteria for all the cast members to celebrate the success of the Spring Festival.

The letdown when it was all over really must have had a big effect on me. I remember tossing and turning all that night in bed, dreaming about the show and all the excitement. I kept waking up feeling so sad that it was over. For months, we had worked up to that big week, and the sudden end to it all reminded me of how I felt when the Knights of Columbus Conventions ended. It was probably partly because I would miss being with Debbi every night.

I did, however, have something new to be excited about, the Junior Prom, which was coming up in a couple of weeks. Debbi and I were going together, and we were doubling with Fred Starno and Peggy Sands. That was going to be a special night. Not only was there a big dance in the gymnasium but there was a post-prom party and dance at a restaurant. We were going to be out until 5 o'clock in the morning. Then we were planning to go to a big prom picnic the next day.

A couple of times, Fred and I got to go out to Wallingford and meet our girlfriends. Over Memorial Day, Debbi had a cookout at her house and invited several people over. Peggy's brother, Jim Sands, was there. He was one of the nicest guys I knew at Notre Dame. He was almost priestly, he was so good. I loved spending time with him. At that picnic, he was smoking a corn cob pipe all day, and I remember all the girls talking about how they liked the smell of his cherry tobacco. Naturally, I had to start smoking a corn cob pipe.

When I told my parents, I was very surprised that they didn't go through the roof. They told me I could smoke the pipe if I wanted to. I picked up the pipe and some cherry tobacco at Soybel's, went home and lit up for the first time. After about ten minutes, I was very dizzy and felt like I was going to throw up any second. Still, it was worth it if Debbi was going to be impressed. I smoked that thing every day for weeks. I hated it.

That wasn't the only time I did something stupid in my quest to be cool. Many of the guys my age were now shaving, and longer sideburns were considered very important to a guy's image. Unfortunately, I hardly had any peach fuzz and kept hoping that a beard would start to develop quickly. My friend from Spring Festival, Andy Nemit, told me his beard-growing secret. In order to spark the growth of whiskers, you needed to sweat. The fastest way to bring this about, he said, was to apply Liquid Heat, a product used to give aching muscles some relief. I thanked him profusely and picked up a bottle of the stuff at Soybel's that afternoon.

That night, I applied the Liquid Heat liberally to my sideburn area, a big BIG mistake! Not only did my beard not develop, but now I had dark red blotches where my sideburns were supposed to be. GREAT idea.

When prom time finally came, Fred and I spent an afternoon washing and waxing his father's old blue car. That night, we drove out to Wallingford and picked up our dates who looked different than we were used to. They were all dressed up in their gowns and had their hair done up on top of their heads. These were not the same girls we had been going out with for so long. We stopped at everyone's home for twenty minutes of picture taking and finally went off to Notre Dame. It didn't even look like our gymnasium. The decorations were unbelievable. The prom just flew by. I remember Fred's car overheating and breaking down on the highway on the way to the post-prom dance but other than that, the whole weekend is a blur.

When my final report card came home in the mail, my parents were furious with some of the poor grades. They told me that I was not going to be able to drive the car, other than to and from Soybel's until I pulled my grades up. The problem was that I wasn't going to get my next report card until the fall of my Senior year. It was going to be next to impossible to have any contact with Debbi that summer.

I was spending more and more time over at Smitty's house. There were lots of people in that neighborhood who were our age. It was about a two-mile walk over to Smitty's, but there always seemed to be plenty going on at the corner of Lake Street and Mather Street. There was a little stone wall there, and we would sit on it many summer days, watching all the girls.

I became interested in one named Priscilla, and being so far away from Debbi and with no transportation to see her, I broke up with her. Priscilla dumped me within a week for some little guy who looked to me like a hoodlum. Great move on my part.

Paradise Park started to have dances each week under the lights of the pavilion on the hill. After years of playing there each summer, it was strange to see all the teenagers up there dancing to the music of a live band. It was like going to a mixer outside.

One band played there quite often. I remember them because they did a great rendition of the Beatles' terrific song, *Hey Bulldog.* That was one of my favorite tunes, and it never came on the radio. I loved when the band played that song so everyone could enjoy what I had liked for so long.

One night was pretty typical of fifteen and sixteen-year-old teenagers: A girl named Susan was after me, but I was interested in a very pretty girl named Dorinda. She was bent on getting back together with her old boyfriend, John. John, in turn, must have been mad at Dorinda for some reason, because he was interested in another girl.

I always thought it would have been fascinating to see what could have happened if John liked Susan. It would have been a great big circle, each one of us chasing someone else. As soon as one stopped, there would have been a big collision.

Through all of this, I kept thinking about how good it would be if I were back with Debbi Merkel. I couldn't believe how stupid I had been in breaking up with her. One day, I decided to sit down and write her a letter telling her how sorry I was and how much she meant to me. By the time I got finished with that letter, I knew there was no way she could want to be away from me.

I sent the letter along with Fred Starno who was still going out with Peggy Sands. He was going to deliver it to her while he was out in Wallingford and I would await the response. It didn't turn out the way it was supposed to.

Fred had the unpleasant task of informing me in great detail what Debbi's reaction was. The bottom line was that she thought I was a big jerk and the letter was a joke. I couldn't help but think how many girls got a big laugh over that letter and vowed that day never to put anything like that in writing. That was the lowest point of the summer.

There were some good distractions, though. I got to go with my family on another Knights of Columbus trip, this time up to Boston for a Board of Directors meeting. I remember the ride in the car. I was traveling with the Griffins, and we kept hearing the song *2525* on the radio. We really liked that song.

Up in Boston for the long weekend, Jim Griffin and I got to go out to Fenway Park and see the Yankees play the Red Sox. Later that night, we were treated to the sight of all of the Yankee players staying in the same hotel with us. That was very exciting.

Also that summer, much of the talk was about the Apollo 11 space mission. Like most people, I was glued to the television set during a lot of that voyage. The day the two astronauts broke away from the mother ship and started their descent down to the moon, I happened to be at Bassett Field with Billy Garcia. His brother was playing baseball, and we were out in his car in the parking lot, listening to the broadcast along with millions of other Americans.

I was holding my breath, listening to the astronaut report back to Houston how he was maneuvering the Lunar craft, coming down ever so slowly until he said he could see the dust coming up. Finally, a crackly voice came over the radio, "Houston, Tranquillity Base here. The Eagle has landed." It was unbelievable.

That night, we stayed up late and watched the ghostly figures in black and white, walking on the surface of the moon. The morning paper had headlines that were almost as big as when Kennedy was shot. In red, white and blue letters, it simply exclaimed, "WE DID IT!".

A couple of other big events happened in the summer of 1969. One was the Woodstock Music Festival in Upstate New York. There were some pictures in the newspaper and some stories on television, but I hardly paid attention to what it was all about. How important could it be if the Beatles weren't there? It wasn't until months later that I even knew that it was one of the biggest events of the decade.

The other thing I remember was the news that there had been some horrible murders committed out in California. A beautiful actress named Sharon Tate had been butchered, along with a bunch of other people. I don't know why, but these stories always grabbed my attention. Not too long after that, America was learning all about Charles Manson and his cult of followers. That was very scary stuff. I read anything I could find on that story.

The rest of the summer was pretty much routine. I "went out" with a few girls, sometimes for as long as two weeks without even seeing them once. I'd negotiate through Smitty, Paula, or another friend to finally get to the girl I was interested in. The message would go out that I liked her, and then we'd have to wait a couple of days for the message to come back as to whether or not she liked me, too. If she did, we were officially boyfriend and girlfriend. The fact that I didn't even know where she lived didn't really seem to matter very much. The important thing was to have a girlfriend. Sometimes, a few days would pass, and the message would come back that she was "breaking up" with me, which was really interesting since we had never been in each other's company even once while we were going out. The breakup details were a critical part of someone's social status. It was much better to be the one who was breaking up as opposed to the one who was being broken up with. I think my record was two-and-two that summer.

The Knights of Columbus held it's Supreme Convention in New Haven that year. Tom Dechant and his family had moved to Connecticut, so I got to see him frequently, not just at conventions. Somehow, this one just didn't have the excitement for me, since I was staying every night in my own house and going to the Park Plaza Hotel each day for the activities. Rosemary was not there, but Jimmy Griffin and I met a couple of girls from Oregon we liked and spent much of the convention with them. My girl had a perfume on that had the scent of apples. I don't remember much else about her.

As the summer wound down, Howie got a book called *Instant Replay* by Jerry Kramer. I borrowed this book from him, and it would eventually become the book I read every night for about a year while I had my three or four bowls of Cheerios. It was the diary of the Green Bay offensive lineman during the 1967 championship season. It covered his intense relationship with coach Vince Lombardi, the horrors of training camp and the challenges of each week's football game. I loved that book. I knew it by heart.

My mother would often ask me why I couldn't spend as much time on my studies as I did on that book or even the Beatles. Once something got my interest, I tended to overdo it.

Chapter Thirteen

1969–1970

Creature Features, "Paul Is Dead" and Prom Breakups

I was back at Notre Dame High School again for my Senior year. I noticed that a lot of the guys had hair bordering on unacceptable as far as the Notre Dame rules were concerned. It seemed that several wanted to show off their new hair on the first day of school before the Brothers told them to make sure it was cut by the following day. The rule was that your ears had to be seen, and any sideburns couldn't go lower than your earlobe. Unfortunately, that was still not a problem for me.

Usually what we did was to allow the very front of our hair to grow as long as possible, keeping it tucked over to one side behind an ear. Then, at the end of the school day, you flipped it loose where it would hang directly in your face, below your nose and almost into your mouth. Most of us looked ridiculous.

Besides hair, there were other quick checks of one's "coolness." Footwear from Barry's Shoes was a must. You had to have loafers that did not have the ripples on the side. Ripples meant that the loafers were not from Barry's. Also, shirts had to be Oxford button downs, usually blue. Ties were wool and very thick. When the weather got colder, it was absolutely imperative that you wear a navy pea coat, and nothing went with that better than a bright blue and white scarf.

I was eagerly awaiting the release of the Beatles' latest album, and it came out that fall. It was called *Abbey Road,* and I picked it up at Cutler's Record Store downtown. On the bus ride home that afternoon, I was looking at the names of the songs and thought them a little strange, even for the Beatles: *Mean Mr. Mustard, Polythene Pam, She Came In Through the Bathroom Window, Maxwell's Silver Hammer* and *Octopus's Garden.* Some of the guys were laughing at me on the bus for picking up the album that day. It turned out to be one of their best.

A week later, I stopped at Cutler's again and bought a pair of drum sticks and a tambourine. I must admit I got pretty good playing the couch with my sticks as I listened to *Abbey Road* at full blast when no one was around.

The first mixer of the year took place on a Friday night, and I went with my friends. I met a pretty girl who was two years younger than me, Gerri Hanley. She was a Sophomore at Hamden High, the public school in my town. We danced all night, and I called her the following week.

I met up with her at the next mixer and started "going out" with her. The problem was, I still couldn't drive the car until I had received a good report card, which was a long way off. Sometimes, I would have to double date with Fred Starno and Peggy Sands. Other times, I would have to walk up to Dixwell Avenue and catch the bus up to the Hamden Plaza, get off and walk a few blocks to her house in the Spring Glenn section of Hamden. I did this on the Saturdays when I didn't have to work.

Gerri and I called these days our "every other Saturday," and I looked forward to them a lot. After meeting with her at her house, we would walk way up to Whitney Avenue and catch a bus to downtown New Haven. There, we would spend most of the day strolling around the Green and shopping in the mall. For lunch, we'd always stop in an Italian restaurant and have a great meal. I would always get the lasagna, which was baked in it's own dish and covered with mozzarella cheese. It was out of this world.

In the middle of the afternoon, we'd bus back to Spring Glenn and walk down Woodlawn Street to her home. There, we'd spend the rest of the afternoon and evening listening to music and playing with the electric guitars and drum set in her basement.

Gerri's parents were two of the nicest people I had ever met and they were wonderful to me. We'd have terrific dinners there every time I visited, and to cap it off, Gerri and I would settle down to watch *Creature Feature*, a Saturday night movie that starred some sort of monster. How I loved "every other Saturdays."

I started to wonder why I was going to an all-boy high school. I really never had thought too much of it before, but now it seemed to be so unnatural to be stuck with hundreds of boys. I couldn't help but think what I was missing by not going to my local high school. I knew I was getting a great formal education at Notre Dame but wondered if I was cheating myself out of a social education, which was an important part of growing up.

Another other thing I remember clearly is sitting in class every day about 10:30 a.m., starving and being overcome with a desire for that lasagna I had with Gerri every other Saturday. I could hardly concentrate on what the teacher was saying, I wanted that cheese so bad.

I started to get away from the long bus ride home every afternoon. A friend from Hamden who was also a St. John's graduate, Jerry Esposito, now had his own car, and I began catching rides with him at the end of the school day. A few of us from Hamden piled in with him every afternoon, chipping in a very small amount each week to help him with money for gas.

The entertainment in the car was Billy Dest. I don't remember him being such a comedian when we went to school together at St. John's, but he was a riot by the time he was a Senior at Notre Dame. He loved to insult everybody, and I didn't mind at all when he started in on me. He was really something.

One day, I was sitting in class, probably thinking about lasagna, when I started to find myself itching a little bit. As time went on, I was itching and scratching more and more. For a while, I thought it was my imagination but I could hardly sit still for three seconds without ten different parts of my body requiring heavy duty scratching.

I was slowly but surely going out of my mind and finally jumped out of my seat and sprinted towards the men's room where I ripped off my shirt and tie and stripped off my tee shirt. I scratched myself for about five or ten minutes, put back on my oxford shirt and tie and tried to make it through the rest of the day.

I don't know what hell is, but I believe I had a little taste of it that day. By the time I got home, I was ready for a straight jacket. My mother thought it was all my imagination until my father got home for supper that evening. He had been going through the same ordeal all day at the office and wanted to know what in the world had happened to him. At least now, I knew I wasn't crazy.

Finally, my mother figured out what the problem was. She had washed or dried some fiberglass curtains in with all our underwear. Apparently, there were thousands of tiny pieces of fiberglass in our clothes, driving my father and me to the brink of madness.

I was still working the usual hours at Soybel's. On lots of occasions, I would get home from work a little after 9:00 p.m. and walk across the street to Billy Garcia's. Billy was finally into the Beatles now and was busy picking up all the albums that had been released over the past few years. It was my job to educate him as to who the lead singer was or what the song was all about. He became a diehard fan.

A story started to circulate around school that there were mysterious clues on Beatles albums over the last couple of years. They were supposed to be evidence that Paul McCartney had died in a car crash and had been replaced with a look alike. The fact that this supposed impostor looked just like Paul, was left handed, played bass guitar and sounded just like him didn't take away from our excitement. It was a treasure hunt for me.

Lots of attention was coming my way at school since I was considered an authority on the subject of the Beatles. Radio stations were now playing Beatle song after Beatle song, updating the listeners on the new clues that were being discovered. For a few days, I was absolutely obsessed with analyzing each of my album covers for *Sergeant Peppers, Magical Mystery Tour, Yellow Submarine, The White Album* and *Abbey Road.* I even used the tea kettle on my stove to steam the blank cover of the *White Album,* hoping against hope that some bizarre message would appear.

One time, Grandma Vivian was over at the house, and I started to go over with her all the clues that I knew about. I will never forget how interested she was, or maybe how much she pretended, but it was a great night together. Grandma had a knack for acting very interested in anything I was excited about. She was always one of my special girls.

Back at school, the talk of the Paul McCartney mystery ended as quickly as it had begun. However, Smitty and I started spending more time between classes with a couple of new friends, Rob Lecza and Rollin Amore. They were two pretty cool guys who loved the Beatles. The four of us would often sing harmony together, putting on many shows for our classmates. That was a lot of fun.

That winter, I started to get into games of pickup hockey. Over near Smitty's house, there was a great place to play, Avis Pond. Hockey was big at Hamden High School, and Smitty knew a lot of the guys who played down at Avis. All I had ever been on in my life were black figure skates, so I had to go out and buy a pair of hockey skates. I could barely stand up on them for a while but I loved those games.

Billy Garcia was also getting into it with some of his friends, so lots of nights I would go over to his house, and we would practice with a tennis ball down in his basement. We hacked away on that tennis ball with our hockey sticks, trying to hit goals into a small doorway. It was terrific playing down there. It was one of the last great times of being a "kid."

It was soon time to sign up for Dancing Knights that January, but most of my attention was outside of Notre

Dame now, and I decided to skip it my Senior year. My girlfriend and most of the guys I was hanging around with, other than Smitty, went to Hamden High School. I couldn't wait to get out.

Sometimes when I'd get home from school at the end of the day, my mother would be watching the soap opera *Another World*. By simply hanging around the TV, I couldn't help but pick up what was going on. I would ask my mother a few questions as to who was good and who was bad and I found myself getting interested in the show. There were three women I remember: Rachel, Iris and Laura. Rachel was pretty evil, but she was my favorite. She was hot. I think she is still doing soap operas today and plays the same type of role. My other favorite was Laura, a beautiful young blonde. I'm not sure, but I think she's famous now. I think it was Donna Mills.

It was about this time that Howie was having trouble at Manhattan College with chest pains. It turned out he had a collapsed lung and needed major surgery. He came home and had an operation and he stayed in the hospital for several days. We went to visit him there, and I remember the poor guy being told by the nurses to lean over and cough. This was apparently important to his recovery. It was extremely painful for him to do this, but nothing compared to when he felt a sneeze coming on. I thought he was going to die when that happened.

Smitty and I started to get into the New Haven Blades, a minor league hockey team that played downtown at the New Haven Arena. There was as much fighting as there was hockey, but they were great nights out. We would see a lot of people we knew and eat tons of junk food.

One night, we got back from a Blades game, and I was going to spend the night sleeping over at Smitty's since we were off from school for a couple of days. We were hanging around his neighborhood when a fellow from down the street came by with a bottle of cherry brandy.

Since we were not going to be in any cars, and it seemed so easy and safe, we helped this guy finish off his pint. By the time I got over to Smitty's house, I was feeling pretty bad. I spent about an hour throwing up in the downstairs bathroom before finally collapsing into bed.

The next day I had a tremendous headache which I guess was part of an official hangover. I never did see what the big excitement was about drinking. It wasn't much fun for me at all.

Uncle Phil died around that time. He was a great guy, and we were all going to miss him. At his wake, I started to think about the good times we all had had when the relatives were together. I remembered how he had given me a hairbrush with my initials, J. F. M., on it for my eighth birthday. I have been using it ever since. There aren't many bristles left, though.

I always liked it a lot when spring would come to New England. The winters were too long, and I always looked forward to the change in season. On the day before Easter, I was over at Gerri's house, and we were playing baseball in her background. It was a beautiful day, and the temperature had to be near sixty. That night, a cold front came through, and we were hit with about a foot of snow for Easter Sunday. It seemed so strange to go back so quickly into winter when just a few hours earlier I was enjoying warm sunshine.

Things were still going a little crazy around the country that spring. Four students were killed at Kent State out in Ohio when the National Guard fired on the demonstrators. Other than liking the Beatles so much, I was very conservative in my political thoughts. I just couldn't understand what everyone was protesting about.

New Haven was the scene of some demonstrations involving the Black Panthers. I think there was a murder in town which allegedly involved members of the Panthers. A few of them were on trial for the crime, and the New Haven Green was the scene of many marches and demonstrations across the street from the courthouse. There were a lot of soldiers and tanks on the outskirts of New Haven for a few days. I guess everyone expected all kinds of trouble, but nothing developed.

The thing that I was most interested in was the breakup of the Beatles. People kept saying that they would get together again, but I knew it was all over. For a while, I thought it might be good to hear all the individual songs that would come out from each of them, but they never did provide the magic for me after that. I guess things never stay the way you want them.

Like most of the other Seniors at Notre Dame, I had applied to several colleges earlier in the year. I really wasn't one of the best students, but that was due to the fact that I pretty much did as little as possible to get decent grades. However, my college boards totaled about 1,250, so I was accepted at the colleges I had applied to. Manhattan College accepted me, the alma mater of both my father and brother. I never really considered going anywhere else once I received the acceptance letter from that school. I planned on attending Manhattan College in the fall.

Gerri and I broke up after the Senior prom. Jim Sands and his girlfriend broke up right after the prom, too. Fred and Peggy broke up soon after, and Peggy started to go out with my good friend, Steve Hammond. Lots of changes occurred after proms.

I was reunited with Debbi Merkel, but ever so briefly. One night, after about an hour of trying to dial her number without shaking, I called her up and asked her if she would like to go to a movie with me that weekend. I was absolutely stunned and ecstatic when she said, "yes." I was a wreck for the next few days in anticipation of our getting back together. The rest of my classmates and friends were thinking about graduation, which was just a week or so away, but I couldn't care less about that.

The big night finally arrived, and I drove out to Wallingford to her house for the first time in a year. When she got in the car, I could hardly open my mouth, I was so nervous, yet tried as hard as I could to show some pride.

We went to a movie at the Strand Theatre in Hamden and we sat there for about twenty minutes watching the movie. I'll never know why this girl got to me so much, but I struggled for probably another twenty minutes, trying to summon the courage to take her hand. I couldn't tell if she was being so quiet because she was as nervous as me or because she just wished she wasn't there at all.

Finally, I reached over and took her hand in mine. I'll never forget how our fingers intertwined and how she gave my hand a nice long squeeze. It was like she was telling me that it was good for us to be back together. It just seemed right. As for me, it was one of the best feelings I have ever had in my life.

No sooner did my heart beat get back close to normal, Debbi excused herself and made a trip to the rest room. When she got back, she sat down and crossed her arms for the rest of the movie. We never said another word. It was like getting hit with a fist right in the stomach.

After I drove all the way back to her house in Wallingford, I stopped in front and planned to walk her up to the door. She just bounced out of the car and said in a real friendly voice, "Thanks a lot, goodnight!" Then she ran up her front steps.

All the way home and for months afterward, I couldn't help wondering why she agreed to go out with me that night. Or how she had the ability to make me feel the way I did.

That summer, I left the part time job at Soybel's and starting working full time down at the Knights of Columbus along with lots of other young people who were on summer break from college. While my father and all the people I knew were already in the twenty-two story office building, a few other guys and I were assigned the task of helping clean up the old building a couple of blocks away. It was a miserable and boring job. I hated it. I was making pretty good money working full-time, but they were long, long, days.

I started bumming cigarettes from some of the older guys I was working with and after a while, began buying my own packs. I smoked Camel filters at first, then moved on to the more popular Marlboros in the flip-top boxes.

Once in a while, I would go up to the "new building" for lunch and was always wishing I could work there. Everyone was all dressed up, and the girls looked lovely. I felt like I was down in the minor leagues and all the fun was up there in the majors.

The only good thing about working full time was that I had every night off. I really looked forward to go-ing over to Steve Hammond's house after supper each evening when we would usually go off to Carvel for "banana barges." Sometimes, we would just play basketball in his driveway and follow that up with a swim in his backyard pool.

I also liked catching rides home from work with one of Howie's friends, Paul Keating. He lived a couple of streets over from us. He was actually just a couple of years older than me but always hung around with my brother's crowd. Paul and I got to be pretty good friends that summer. The one thing I remember about those rides home was singing with him at the top of our lungs to a new song that had come out by the Temptations called *Ball of Confusion*. The problem was that Paul and I would really butcher the words to the song. For a couple of years, I really thought the name of the song was *All of the Children*.

That August, it was time for the annual convention for the Knights of Columbus, which was to be my last one. It was in Houston, Texas, and I was very excited about the prospect of seeing Rosemary. We were still writing to each other regularly, and she told me that she and her family were attending.

I met her one night at her hotel and was shocked by how good she looked. She had changed a lot in two years, but had only become prettier, if that was possible. I had assumed that we were going to be spending the week together but I sensed right from the beginning that it was going to be different. She was real nice and friendly but seemed to just want to be part of a large group. It wasn't like we were going to be a special couple on that convention.

I remember dancing with her a few times at the teen functions, but she was also dancing with lots of other guys as well. We never did spend any time alone, and I couldn't figure out what was wrong. I had a pretty good time in

Houston but couldn't shake off the disappointment I felt about Rosemary.

It wasn't until the last night that I understood what was going on. About half way through the dance, she asked me if I would walk her back to her hotel, which I did. On the way, she explained to me that she had a boyfriend back home and felt funny about being with me at the convention. By the time we finished talking, things were as good as they were two years earlier in Disneyland. She was in my arms for a long time and all those great feelings l had came roaring back over me. I couldn't help but feel that we had wasted a week but I guess that's the way she wanted it to be. I walked back to my hotel that night in the same daze I had known in California. We wrote to each other for another year or so, but I never saw her again.

The convention was almost over, but there were a few families still around for another day or so. On the night before we flew back to Connecticut, I joined up with a bunch of kids sitting around the swimming pool. One of the girls had an acoustic guitar and was playing songs for us. We were all singing along, and I started to harmonize with the guitar player. I must admit we sounded pretty good and I had a real nice evening singing with her. I vowed to get a guitar as soon as I got home, which I did. I taught myself some cords and played that guitar for several years.

I remember getting back from the convention with only one week to go before starting my Freshman year at Manhattan College. I was planning to not work that week, but my father told me that I was needed. There I was, just coming off an all expense-paid vacation, and throwing a fit because I had to work another week. I was furious, but it didn't do any good. I don't know why it bothered me so much that I had to work. Maybe I just wanted to be a kid with no responsibilities for just a few more days. Sounds familiar.

Chapter Fourteen

1970–1971

Manhattan College

y parents drove me down to Manhattan College right after Labor Day, and we moved all my stuff into Jasper Hall, the dormitory where I was going to be living. My roommate had not yet arrived and when my parents said good-bye to me, I remember just sitting there all alone. It only lasted about an hour or so before I met some other guys, but I'll never forget how homesick I felt sitting there in that room by myself. I wanted so badly to be back in my house on Furman Road, preferably nine years old again.

My roommate turned out to be a nice guy from Huntington Station, Long Island. His name was Joe Daley. We were on the second floor of a five story dormitory. There were a few rooms that had other Freshmen in it, but the majority of students on our floor were Sophomores.

These guys turned out to be some of the most amazing people I had ever met in my life.

Many of them were from Long Island, but there were also a few from Brooklyn, and they were a lot more worldly than anyone else I had known up until that point. Compared to these guys, I had led a very sheltered Beaver Cleaver life up in Connecticut. I don't know if I ever got used to those college students.

Pete and Woody lived next door, and they were a couple of good guys who had a terrific stereo system set up in their room. Across the hall, Jack and Joe, also Sophomores, were also good guys. They were a little more mature than the others, had serious girlfriends and were bent on getting good grades and good careers. Terry and Jim lived further down the hall. Terry was a big tall fellow with a trimmed beard who loved to listen to old-fashioned big band music. Jim was the guy who seemed to know more about politics and government that anyone else I had ever known. He was constantly talking about the war in Vietnam. In fact, I learned more about what was going on in Vietnam in those first few weeks than I had learned in all the years before. Some guys were obsessed with what was going on over there.

By far and away, the two most entertaining students in all of Jasper Hall had to be Joe McGuire and his roommate, Jay Hezlan, also known as "The Oim." Joe was a great swimmer on the college team, had a tremendous sense of humor and was probably the most popular guy on the floor. His roommate, Jay, was also extremely funny, but in a Brooklyn, insulting way. He would squint out from behind his granny glasses and take apart anyone in order to get some laughs. Needless to say, I made sure I stayed on his good side.

I became very friendly with a Freshman from Upstate New York near Buffalo. His name was Bill Harding, but he was known as "William F." He pretty much had the same type of background as me, and we became close friends right from the start.

As far as college life was concerned, it took a little while to get used to the daily routine. Sometimes, you had a class at 8:30 in the morning and would not have another one until 1:00 in the afternoon. Usually, you hung around the cafeteria between classes and tried to catch up on your studies.

Manhattan College was supposed to be an all-boy Catholic school, but we had a "sister school" a few miles away called the College of Mount Saint Vincent. We were starting to combine some classes with the girls from that school, and I remember having Biology at Mount Saint Vincent that year. That took some time for me to get used to. After four years of an all-boy high school, I was distracted, to say the least, with girls in my class. One time, a beauty crossed her legs just to the side of me. It was all I could do to not elbow my friend and whisper, "Look! A leg with no hair!"

Every weekend was a huge party across the campus. The legal age for drinking in New York was only eighteen, so no one had to hide what they were doing. These parties would go until the wee hours of the morning, and music would be blaring everywhere. The next mornings were always the same. All you could smell was spilled stale beer and the remains of the throw up from people who were sick as dogs from drinking too much.

Sometimes, Bill Harding and I liked to get away from the campus and the beer blasts on the weekend. Manhattan College was actually way up on the west side of the Bronx near Broadway and 242nd Street. We'd walk down the 110 steps from campus to the Irish neighborhood on Broadway and catch the El to Times Square. This trip was always a new adventure for me. We'd be on a graffiti-covered subway car and slowly move out of the Bronx through Harlem and into Manhattan. Street people and beggars seemed to be everywhere. We learned quickly not to speak to anyone who approached us. Sometimes, we'd stay down there until 3:00 in the morning going to movies and eating hot-dogs at the little restaurants.

I remember one night we saw both *Mash* and *Patton* at the same theater. *Mash* was getting all the attention at college, but I liked *Patton* a lot more. I guess I still like the traditional movies where America comes out on top.

When Bill and I rode the subway from the city up to campus, we were always a little bit apprehensive. Most people who rode the New York City subway system at 3:00 in the morning were not the kind of people we were used to being around. I will always remember what a good feeling it was when the train came out of the tunnel and turned into the El up in the Bronx, and we could see the Manhattan College chapel tower way off in the distance up on the hill. It was almost like an old lighthouse in the distance helping to bring us home.

I turned eighteen years old that October and by law, had to get my military draft card. That was something that seemed to bother a lot of the guys at school, but it really had no impact on me. I just did what I was supposed to do and didn't think too much of it. Not too long after that, the government went with a lottery system for the draft, and everyone was on edge to see what number he would get. I ended up with something in the 150s.

During the school week, I stayed busy going to classes and trying to keep up with my homework. Stereos would be pumping out music from almost every room during the evening. I started learning more about other rock and roll groups that I had ignored for years. The most popular band seemed to be the Rolling Stones, especially one of their live albums. All the singers who had been at Woodstock were also big at school, especially Joe Cocker. As for me, I just couldn't figure out how anyone could think that all this music could even compare to the Beatles. I just didn't get it.

Manhattan College did not have big time football but did have a Football Club. On some Saturdays, we would play other colleges who had the same sort of club. Fordham was located somewhere near the Bronx Zoo, and its team was our biggest rival. Football games on Saturday afternoon were pretty good, but they were small time. I often wondered what it was like to go to a big school.

There was usually a big mixer every couple of weeks. It would be centered in the main cafeteria building and have three bands. One would be playing on the second floor, one would be playing on the first floor, and usually a couple of folk singers would be down in the lower level. These dances were a lot wilder than what I was used to at Notre Dame High School. Draft beer was served everywhere, and it didn't take long for everyone to be in a partying mood.

I met a pretty high school Senior from Yonkers who would come down to Manhattan College with her friends for the big mixers. Pretty soon, she began coming by herself to meet up with me.

I was a little nervous about Janet being around some of my Sophomore buddies. She was a beauty but a little innocent compared to these guys. However, they all had their girlfriends with them at these dances and were very polite. Even Jay Hezlan was the perfect gentleman.

My brother was now engaged to a great girl named Mary Ellen Lee. One time, they drove down to school for Homecoming, and Janet and I doubled with them. We all went to the football game together and a big dance that night. That was pretty cool, doubling with my older brother after all those years.

One night that fall, I received a telephone call from Smitty up in Connecticut. His sister Doreen was getting married that weekend, and I had promised a long time ago that I would be there for the wedding. I had to hustle to get up to Connecticut that Friday afternoon, catching a train from Grand Central Station up to New Haven.

By this time, my family had moved from Furman Road out to the Mount Carmel section of Hamden, on a street called Breezy Court. This was my first trip "home" and I found myself in a strange house. I had been so busy away at college that it had never really sunk in that the family had moved from the house I had lived in for eighteen years. The new home was much bigger and much nicer. It seemed like a mansion. But I hated not being back on Furman Road.

The first thing I noticed was that there was no stream of people coming in and out all day. At Furman Road, my friends were always coming and going. So were Howie's pals. Even Maureen and all her little friends were always over at our house. We were way out by ourselves now. It didn't seem right.

Back at Manhattan College we had a tradition on Wednesday nights. It was called "over the hump night" and it was almost as big a party night as Friday or Saturday.

They had two bars down the hill called The Green Leaf and The Pinewood. These were two taverns that all the students frequented. They had Manhattan College banners and mugs as part of the decor. On Wednesday nights, there were lines of people outside both these places, waiting to get in. Lots of girls from Mount St. Vincent and Elizabeth Seton College up in Yonkers came, too. Wednesday was an important night for getting a date for the upcoming weekend.

I returned home to Connecticut again for Thanksgiving. It was a custom for the recent Notre Dame graduates to attend the Green Bowl on Thanksgiving morning, the football game between Hamden High and Notre Dame. That was a lot of fun.

Thanksgiving dinner itself was different now. Uncle Phil was gone, but it was still great seeing Grandma and Aunt Cha. That night, Smitty and I went to the traditional mixer back at Notre Dame. It was fun to see the old Brothers and other teachers who were there. It was strange seeing everybody drink Cokes all night after having draft beer at all the other dances I had been to in the last few months. I met a Senior from St. Mary's High School that night, and she was very interested in what college life was all about. I spent the evening dancing with her but never called her.

At school, my hair was getting longer than ever. I hadn't had it cut since the summer and for some reason, I was anxious to show it off for the long semester break at Christmas. I finally had a good stubble of whiskers on my chin and was anxious to show that off as well, even though it was pretty seedy looking.

Final exams took place about a week before Christmas, and I couldn't wait for the semester to end. The weather turned very cold, and we had a big snow storm one night. That just made me want to get back to Connecticut as soon as I could. I was counting the days.

When exams finally ended, I was on the train back to Connecticut for a five-week break. Christmas was wonderful, but I remember getting a haircut that almost ruined everything. I guess I wasn't paying attention when I was sitting in the barber's chair, and he took off just about everything I had worked so hard to grow for so many months. Mom and Dad thought I looked great, but I was almost ashamed to leave the house. Hair was critical in those days, and I was humiliated with the short haircut I now had.

That New Year's Eve, I joined Smitty and some other people for a party. Because we were still three years away from the legal drinking age in Connecticut, we went down in the woods near Smitty's house and drank beer. It had to be about ten degrees that night, and there I was standing next to a frozen lake shivering while I drank.

After drinking legally out in the open at college, I found this to be absolutely appalling. I was just not used to sneaking around like a child after my experiences in the big city. After about an hour of pontificating and complaining, my friends pretty much told me to shut up. After midnight, Smitty and I walked back to his house, and I spent the night there. We were always smart enough not to get in a car after drinking a few beers.

For the next few weeks, I worked again at the Knights of Columbus, this time over in their printing plant, the Supply Department. A few of us college students began working for Mr. John Bowden. Among others, I worked with Tom Dechant and Bill Howard, a great guy who was probably three years older than me. He was one of the funniest people I had ever met, and we had a terrific time working together.

Mr. Bowden had been a Major in the Army years earlier, so we affectionately referred to him as "The Major."

He ran that supply operation like he was still in the military, and we went right along with him. We would answer him, "Yes, sir!", snap a salute and stand at attention whenever he talked to us. It wasn't like we were having fun at his expense. We truly loved the man, and I think he enjoyed all the attention. He played the game right along with us.

During that long semester break, Smitty and I went with a few friends to see Ryan O'Neal and Ali MacGraw in *Love Story*. That silly little movie really got to me. Ali MacGraw looked and acted a lot like Debbi Merkel. It just about crushed me when her character was dying at the end of the movie.

I returned to Manhattan College to begin my second semester. One night we heard a lot of laughing coming from the recreation room. Some of us went in to see what was going on, and there were about thirty guys gathered around the television set. One was yelling out, "This is like watching my own father!" It turned out to be Archie Bunker and the debut of *All In the Family*. It was a great hit among the college students. I really enjoyed it.

I also remember going to a movie that was being shown on campus one night. We were all packed in, ready to see an old film called *Freaks*. I guess it was sort of a cult classic, featuring some midgets and really bizarre characters from the circus sideshows. Everyone was having a wild time, shouting up things at the characters in the movie. It was one of the funniest nights at school that year. I'll never forget the cheers of the audience when the "freaks" went on a rampage at the end of the movie, seeking revenge on the villains who had treated them badly. I couldn't believe an old movie could generate so much excitement on a college campus.

Even though football was small time at Manhattan, the basketball program was just the opposite. The team had been to the NCAA tournament when my brother was there, and I got a taste of going to games downtown at Madison Square Garden.

Some of the biggest college basketball teams visited The Garden to play Manhattan during the school week. Usually, it was a double-header, so I always got to see two other big-name teams as well. The students always sat together on the floor behind the basket. The biggest basketball game of the year, for us, was when we played our arch rival, Fordham University. Hundreds of us walked down the stairs from the campus to Broadway and 242nd Street and caught the El to downtown. We marched through the streets to Madison Square Garden singing college fight songs. People on the streets would move out of the way while we all stopped traffic during our march. I guess it was part of the exciting tradition each year.

That spring, I met a Freshman girl from Elizabeth Seton College who was part of a crowd that hung around with some of the Sophomores on my floor. She came to one of the dances at Manhattan. I remember some of her friends were part of the hippie crowd, which was kind of new to me. We danced a few times that night, and everyone went back to the dormitory to continue partying. We sat up all night just talking and talking. We got together a couple of more times, and I really liked being with her. Her name was Anne McCarthy.

Just when the semester was about to end, I went up to Yonkers and spent an afternoon and evening with her. We were both going home that weekend, so it would be the last time I would see her for a while. It was a great day just strolling around her campus together, but I was already missing her.

When I returned home to Connecticut, I started my summer job again at the Knights of Columbus. This time, however, I was thrilled to hear that I would be working in the big building, helping out the boys in the mailroom. They were pretty much all old-timers who worked in the basement, sorting out the in-coming mail and delivering it throughout the building. Many of them had vacation plans, so I guess it was a good time to have a couple of extra people down there for the summer. I was thrilled when Paul Keating joined me as the other summer addition.

We had a ball! Paul and I just hit it off perfectly with the guys in the mailroom. Mr. Murray was the boss, sitting over by his desk barking out his orders. He was always yelling at Paul and me because we were cutting up so much, but I think he started to think of us as his sons, and we had a great time working for him. There was one young fellow there named Sal, but the others were pretty close to retirement: Joe, Charlie and Frank.

Frank McCaully turned out to be one of the funniest people that Paul and I had ever met. He was a little Irishman who just loved to get on Paul and me. We played up to him and were perfect victims for all his cracks and insults. Throughout the day, we would leave the basement with our little shopping carts to go on the "runs" throughout the twenty-two story building. This would usually take about fifteen minutes for the others, but Paul and I would stop and socialize with everyone we met, sometimes not returning for forty-five minutes. Frank would always be sitting there and when we finally got back, he would mumble, "Where have you guys been, Brooklyn?" For some reason, everyone else in the mailroom thought this was great comedy, and Paul and I would die laughing just watching the response from all the others. We would always pretend we were shocked and hurt by Frank's insults, which naturally made him keep it up even more.

It turned out that Frank McCaully only lived a few blocks from Paul, so sometimes we stopped over at his house on Saturday afternoons with a couple of six packs. We sat in his back yard while his wife made us something to eat. I think Frank really enjoyed the fact that a couple of college guys were taking the time to see him, but he'd just keep up the pretense that we were nothing but a couple of lazy bums. We teased him about his bald head and he swore at us, his blue eyes twinkling all the time. He always had a Benson and Hedges cigarette hanging out of his mouth. Boy, how we loved that guy.

For some reason, I was obsessed with getting a great tan that summer. We'd go down to Anchor Beach in Milford and spend hours there lying in the sun, trying to get that perfect tan. I really overdid it one day, thinking that my sunburn would slowly turn into a nice bronze color. I'll never forget how I was up all night peeling strips of flesh from my chest, in more pain than I had ever known. I swear I had second-degree burns. I kept vowing over and over not to do anything like that again as long as I lived.

One day, I had to catch a train from New Haven to school to get some information on going to summer school at the University of New Haven. I had failed a French class and needed some stuff from my teacher to give to the University. While I was visiting the campus, who did I run into but Anne McCarthy and some of her friends? This had not been planned at all, and it was a nice surprise to see her again. I ended up calling my parents and telling them I wouldn't be home until late that night. I was going out to Long Island to spend the rest of the day and evening with Anne at her home.

I had a terrific time with her and her family but had a long trip back home in front of me. I don't think I got into the train station in New Haven until about three o'clock the next morning.

Soon I was back in the mailroom, half asleep. Naturally, Frank McCaully and the boys really got on my case. Frank couldn't believe that the encounter was just a coincidence. He was certain that the whole thing had been planned for weeks. All day long, he kept giving me special projects to do when all I wanted was to put my head down on the table and go to sleep.

As much as I loved going to work each day, I was really enjoying every evening that summer, too. Smitty and I, looking for something to do, started to get into pinball at the Hamden Duck Pin Bowling Lanes. He and I would play the same machine over and over again. It cost a quarter for three games, and we got so good we stood there and played for hours on the same quarter. Free balls and free games just kept coming and coming while we took turns at the machine. I still played that game in my head when I tried to fall asleep at night.

Meanwhile, I was also finding time to practice on the guitar I had bought a year earlier. I had been playing that thing every day since I bought it and could now play about twelve different chords. This range allowed me to play pretty much anything I wanted to by Bob Dylan. It was also easy to play the chords of several songs by Crosby,

Stills, Nash and Young. Neil Young's songs were by far the easiest to learn. Beatles' songs weren't as simple, except for a handful. *You've Got To Hide Your Love Away* was my favorite on the acoustic guitar.

Anne McCarthy and her family invited me down to Long Island for a long weekend, and she wanted me to bring my guitar along. She always liked listening to me sing. I remember singing John Lennon's *A Working Class Hero*. The weather was gorgeous that weekend, and we got in her car and went out to Long Beach for the day. It was perfect, just holding her hand and strolling up and down the beach that day. We made plans for Anne to come up to Connecticut in August to go to Yale Bowl with me for one of the pop concerts that were popular then. The Who was going to be performing, and I had two tickets.

Unfortunately, a couple of weeks before The Who concert, there was a lot of trouble and fights at another show, so the remaining summer concerts were canceled. I was extremely disappointed with that. I couldn't believe that a few jerks had spoiled my plans.

Howie and Mary Ellen got married that August, and I was the best man. I did one of the readings and was pretty nervous, but managed to pull it off.

All our relatives and lots of Howie's friends were there, and we all went out to the reception. When we got there, we learned that another wedding reception was in another section of the restaurant. We couldn't believe it, but who did we see in the bar, Benson and Hedges hanging from his mouth, but Frank McCaully? He was at the wedding of a nephew.

Paul Keating and I were thrilled. We got Frank to spend most of his time with us at Howie's reception. All of our friends could finally see for themselves what Paul and I had been talking about all summer. They all became instant Frank McCaully fans. I'll never forget how he was dancing a slow dance with Paul's sister, Chris.

The other big thing that happened that day was when a waitress at the restaurant came over to me and said, "Hi, Jim. How are you?" I looked up and there was Debbi Merkel, as friendly and beautiful as ever. I don't know if I even choked out a response. I pretty much went into a catatonic state and nodded my head a few times.

Here I was, a college man, all dressed up in a tuxedo and handling all the responsibilities of being the best man. But Debbi could turn me instantly into a blithering idiot. I had come a long way.

There were to be no more Knights of Columbus Conventions for me. I was now working each summer and too old for that kind of stuff. The convention was in New York City that year and Mom, Dad and Maureen went without me.

I got a big kick out of watching TV one night. President Nixon was the main speaker at the convention's State Dinner, and the newscasts were showing parts of the speech. Right behind him, sitting at the head table in his white tuxedo was my father. That was pretty exciting for me to see. Dad was also on the front page of some newspapers the next morning, right there behind the President.

With summer winding down, everyone was packing up and making plans to go back to school.

Chapter Fifteen

1971–1972

Flunking Out, The Olympics and Broadcasting School

I began my Sophomore year that September, rooming with Bill Harding. We were still on the second floor of Jasper Hall, but had a different room. During the first week, we found an old couch down on Broadway that a family was throwing out with their trash. We thought it would be perfect for our room and dragged it up the stairs to campus. It was filthy, and the legs were broken off, but it matched our decor.

We started spending a lot of time with a couple of guys named Tom Blackburn and Tom O'Neil. Blackburn was on the swimming team, a big, fun guy with blonde hair. O'Neil was from Staten Island, and this was his first year living on campus. He was the real ladies' man in the group. He was also very funny.

One weekend early in the school year, the three of them came back to Connecticut for the weekend with me.

It was fun introducing them to my family and friends. My two different worlds came together for a couple of days.

By this time, Smitty was going out with a Hamden girl named Dale Stradley. She had a friend named Karen Weiss who was probably one of the prettiest girls I had ever known. She looked a little like Michelle Phillips from the Mamas and Papas. I remember hot pants were popular that year, and I saw them for the first time on Karen. She was a sight to behold. You were never sure how a weekend would turn out when you brought different friends together, but everyone got along fine. We had a great time in Connecticut.

Back at school, I ran into Anne McCarthy a couple of times, but had met a couple of other girls, too. I started going out with a girl named Lucy from Elizabeth Seton. We went out every weekend for a month or so. One time, we went to a big ball down in the city. We doubled with Tom Blackburn and his date. I liked Lucy but remember being a little intimidated by how much she could drink. It didn't seem to bother her a bit.

A couple of weeks later, it was "over the hump" night, and I was down at the Pinewood with my buddies. There was a pretty girl there, laughing and vivacious. I must have had enough beers in me to feel pretty confident because the next thing I knew, I was sitting with her on top of one of the booths, talking with her and getting her phone number.

She also went to Elizabeth Seton College, and I called her the next night. When a girl answered at her dormitory, she recognized me and assumed I wanted to talk to Lucy. I said, no, I wanted Mary Beth, the girl I had met the night before. I remember hearing a lot of whispering and talking in the background through the phone. It turned out that Lucy and Mary Beth lived on the same floor. I finally got a hold of Mary Beth, and we made plans to go to a dance that weekend at Manhattan.

When I got off the phone, I couldn't help but wonder what Lucy must have thought that night. It's funny how when you don't care for a girl anymore, it seems easy to move on. But when she doesn't care for you, it stays with you for so long. I thought of all the girls I ended relationships with and wondered if they felt the same way as I did when I was dumped. I'm sure these things pretty much even out over a lifetime, but it always seems that you dwell on the girls who don't want you.

Bill Harding came home with me for the Thanksgiving holidays. It was great having him there with my family and showing him all the sights of my home town. He had never enjoyed a real lobster roll in Upstate New York. He had tasted lobster salad, but that was with mayonnaise. Now he got a chance to sample pieces of lobster drenched in butter on a grilled bun. Bill thought he was in heaven.

We also went to the Notre Dame mixer on Thanksgiving night, and he really enjoyed that as well. We had a great time together those few days in November. We almost hated to have to go back to school on Sunday afternoon.

Bill and I started staying up later and later each night, enjoying the late shows on TV. It was getting harder and harder to get up for early morning classes, but I knew I had to buckle down for final exams. I had a lot of catching up to do, so I barely got passing grades that semester. Cs and Ds were all over my report card. I was looking forward to the spring semester when I would bounce back and really get into my studies.

Over the Christmas holidays and long semester break, I spent all my time with Smitty, Dale and Karen. Karen was more beautiful than ever. She was sort of my date during those weeks, and I loved going anywhere with her. One time, we went to a New Haven Blades hockey game, and there were several guys there from the Knights of Columbus summers and Christmas crew. I was never more proud than I was that night, holding her hand and walking around the arena in front of all my friends. I knew even then that showing off a "trophy girl" was a little lame but I couldn't help myself. She was that striking.

Aside from that, I enjoyed it even more when I was alone with her. She was an angel underneath those good looks. One night, we sat up quite late discussing religion and other heavy things. I loved talking to her.

That was a bitter cold winter. Sometimes, the four of us would go ice skating at Brooksvale Park. It had to be zero degrees there a couple of nights, but we had a great time. Sometimes my hands were so cold even with the gloves, I could hardly untie my skates and get them off at the end of the night. My lips were so chapped that they were cracked and bleeding for several days. I worried about how good my kisses were.

On New Year's Eve, Smitty, Dale, Karen and I went out to dinner at Riley's Restaurant on Whitney Avenue. Afterwards, we drove around in my mother's '66 red Chevy. We ended up parking next to the bean field in my old neighborhood and started singing along with the music on the radio. Smitty and I could actually harmonize pretty well together and eventually started entertaining the girls with some of our Beatles' selections. *Nowhere Man* was one of our best, as well as *If I Fell.* It was a great New Year's Eve.

Back at Manhattan College again for the second semester, I couldn't help but see a dramatic change in the personality of our friend, Tom O'Neil. He was now spending more time with Jay Hezlan and some of his pals. Tom didn't seem to want to spend any more time with Bill and me. When we did run into him, he was still very funny, but now his sense of humor was as cynical and biting as Jay's. I really missed the old Tom O'Neil.

In the first semester, Tom and I had played pool and ping pong for hours. I was considered one of the best ping pong players in the dormitory. I guess all my hundreds of hours practicing in the basement on Furman Road paid off. Tom and I used to put on some good shows in front of the other students, sometimes standing ten or fifteen feet from the edge of the table, slamming that ball back and forth. He wasn't interested in doing that anymore. I never did figure out what happened there.

Meanwhile, I was not living up to my vow to get into my studies that semester. I kept putting off homework and classes the first week. Usually, there was a lot of confusion the first few days of a semester while students were changing classes and running over to one of the buildings to register for different courses. I guess I thought with all the chaos, I could get away with all the slacking off and really get into it after a week or so but I started off way behind.

Bill and I continued our habit of staying up later and later, watching one late show after another. I knew I was headed toward trouble but I was having so much fun and I was also just plain lazy. I was always planning to work hard the next day.

We did everything but our homework. I think we were just slipping back into childhood. Sometimes, several of us would go up to the fifth floor to Tom Blackburn's room. We got into this game where we made elaborate paper airplanes and sent them out the windows of his room, competing with each other as to how far they would fly before they hit the ground. Bill always outdid us. He would tape a couple of bottle rockets to the wings of the airplane, lighting both fuses before sending it out the window. It was fun to watch this thing soar out for a few seconds, then explode in rockets. We were a bunch of nineteen-year-olds, acting like we were still ten.

By now, I was falling so far behind I wondered if I could ever catch up with my studies. I was turning into such a bum that I was getting dirty and skinny. I never got up in time for breakfast and probably missed a lot of lunches, as well. I needed something to pull myself up.

One day, I heard about a big Beatles' special that was going to be on the Manhattan College radio station that night. One of the disc jockeys knew I was quite a fan and sort of an authority on their music. He asked me if I would stop in at the station and help them on the air. I wasn't sure about this but said I would come by.

That night, I went over to the radio station on campus and watched a couple of the disc jockeys play the Beatles' music and talk about their songs. Once in a while, the phone would ring with requests from the students. Eventually, they put some ear-phones on me and put a microphone in front of my face. I started to talk about some of the songs that were being played, how they were written and what some of the background stories were. Pretty soon, the phone started ringing over and over again with people asking me to play different songs and asking me questions about what some of the verses meant. I had a ball that night. I really felt like a celebrity, answering all the questions and playing all the great music. I started to think that maybe *this* was something I could be good at. Maybe even a job was possible in the radio business.

The next day, everyone was stopping me and telling me how much they enjoyed my "show" the night before. My thoughts started to turn even more toward a career in broadcasting. I had heard of schools for that kind of thing when I was in Connecticut. Maybe this was the answer I was looking for. Since I was obviously going to flunk out of Manhattan, maybe I could hang my hat on something new. Suddenly, broadcasting school was what was going to get me back into the swing of things.

A few days before Easter break, I came down with a sore throat. It got so bad over the next couple of days that I couldn't even swallow. I had had sore throats before but nothing like this. I ended up going to the infirmary, and the doctors gave me some medicine, but I was as sick as a dog. Instead of my taking the train home for Easter, my parents came to get me.

Back in Connecticut, I went to the family doctor who concluded that I had strep throat and put me on a stronger prescription. While I was recuperating, and still being pampered, I thought it was the perfect time to start hinting to Mom and Dad that I was thinking about making a change in schools for the fall. When they didn't seem terribly upset by what I was suggesting, I kept talking and talking about how much I wanted to go to the Connecticut School of Broadcasting. I further explained that since this was a rather dramatic change, I felt that I should pay for all of the tuition costs. I think my parents knew how badly I was doing at Manhattan, so maybe they were a little relieved that I would be continuing some sort of education.

Suddenly, my worries were over. I knew I was now going to become focused on something that meant a lot to me. I was going to go to Broadcasting School, become a disc jockey and start a wonderful career in radio.

There were just a few short weeks remaining at college when I got back after Easter. Bill Harding was also flunking out, ending his days at Manhattan College, and we would sit up each night talking about what we were going to do the following fall. He was going to get involved in something up near his home and was just as excited about that as I was about my decision. I think we were both happy to get a new start on life.

One night, I got a call from Smitty back in Connecticut. He had been going to the University of New Haven but, like me, he was not doing all that well. He had left school and, unfortunately, had a very low number in the draft lottery. He now informed me that he was going into the Army.

So many things were going on that spring that I could hardly stop to think about what was taking place. The war in Vietnam was winding down. The troops were returning, but I still couldn't picture my best friend not being there when I got home. In a way, though, I think Smitty was a little bit relieved to know what he would be doing for the next couple of years. I guess we were both grasping onto something . . . anything.

The summer of '72 was something I had been looking forward to for a long, long time. I never thought that it could match the great summer of '71 but I was wrong. It turned out to be the best summer ever.

It was back to basics for me. I was eating my mother's home-cooked meals every night. I was getting up early every morning to go to work at the Knights of Columbus. I was wearing clean clothes and taking a shower every day. Basically, I was living a normal life.

When I learned that Paul Keating and I were slated again to work down in the mailroom, I couldn't believe my good fortune. Another summer vacation with Frank McCaully and the boys. It was too good to be true!

All the same old jokes, all the teasing and insults, all the laughs started up on the very first day. We all played pinochle every lunch hour and got pizzas at Pepe's Restaurant down on Wooster Street. Paul and I still made our "runs" delivering and picking up the mail. There were so many great people on all those floors that sometimes it took me forever to get back downstairs. I loved to stop and visit with everyone. Sure enough, Frank would always ask where I had been, *"Brooklyn?"* Some things never change.

Outside the mailroom in the lower level there was an underground parking area for the executives. There were also a couple of loading docks there for truck deliveries. The man who was stationed at The Door was quite a character named Tom Bove. He was pretty close to retirement and for some reason, took every Monday and Tuesday off. On those days I was promoted to The Door. This was a great job, too. I would sit there at the desk reading the newspaper or a book and asking each person who came in where they were going. They usually had to sign in on a clipboard at my desk.

I found an old steel bar over in the corner and started to do exercises with it each day. It probably only weighed about fifteen or twenty pounds but it was perfect for doing one-handed curls. Within a few weeks, my biceps were getting bigger and bigger. Between this and eating more, I began to put on some badly-needed weight that summer. I was clean, healthy and tan with short hair and a suit and tie. I felt like a million bucks.

I was even using my mind a little more, too. After months of staring at the television and playing with paper airplanes, I really got into reading that summer. My work at The Door allowed me to get through several books. My favorite was one that Jim Sands lent to me, *One Flew Over the Cuckoo's Nest.* I thought that was an absolute classic.

On Saturdays, Paul and I would join up with a couple, Bobby and Janice, pile into his car and head up to Misquamicut Beach in Rhode Island. I remember the weather being beautiful every weekend, and we would get up there early in the morning to swim and work on our tans. Usually, by about noon time, Paul and I left Bobby and Janice to themselves and headed over to the local bar called The Wreck. It was kind of a motorcycle gang hangout, but I'm sure Paul and I were not a threat to these guys. We minded our own business, and no one ever bothered us. Since we didn't have to worry about driving, we would usually stay in there a couple of hours, drinking pitchers of beer. When we joined Bobby and Janice for the ride back home, we had to ask them about every twenty minutes to stop and let us go to the bathroom.

With Smitty off in the Army, I was spending all of my time with Paul and the rest of Howie's crowd. Sometimes, we would all go down to Paul's Uncle Tommy's in Milford. He and Aunt Jo had a great swimming pool in their backyard and loved having the big crowd down on Sundays. Uncle Tommy was a real character just like all the Keatings. We had some great cookouts with him.

I remember hearing the comedian George Carlin that summer. He had an album out that I thought was the funniest thing I had ever heard. I even made my father sit down one night and listen to the record. Although Carlin was a "hippie" in my father's eyes, even he found himself getting some big laughs from the routines.

I applied to the Connecticut School of Broadcasting as planned. I had to go through an audition and bought a light blue blazer and new tie for the occasion. Everyone else was dressed in casual clothes. I don't know why I thought I was supposed to be so formal. I waited nervously for a couple of weeks until I received my letter of acceptance.

At this point, I was just thrilled to be able to tell people that yes, I was going back to school in the fall. It was just a different type of school. I think going to Broadcasting School was sort of a crutch for me that summer. I had it in my mind that I was going back to school just like all my friends. It wasn't until the end of the summer that I realized everything was going to be different.

The summer was going by much too quickly. Every day at work was fun and hanging around with Paul and my new group of friends was a blast. For some crazy reason, we started to watch the old re-runs of the *Superman* series starring George Reeves. It was almost like a cult because so many of us gathered around the television set at Paul's house, hooting and hollering along with the dialog. We knew those old shows by heart and really had a good time watching them.

Sometimes, I would go with my family out to Seymour in The Valley to enjoy cookouts at my Uncle George and Aunt Betty's. They had a swimming pool, and we had a lot of fun out there. I remember the game of Jarts was popular then, and we'd play that game for hours during those afternoons. Uncle Frank and Aunt Vern would come by once in a while, too.

A couple of other things got my attention that summer. I remember reading about a break-in at the Democratic Headquarters in Washington, DC. There were rumors coming out that some of President Nixon's people had been involved in it or at least in a cover-up. Not much actually came to the surface right away, but I had a feeling this thing called "Watergate" was going to be big.

The Summer Olympics began in Munich, Germany that year. We were glued to our television sets, watching the Russian gymnast, Olga Korbet, perform her wonderful routines. She was a little doll, and America fell in love with her. Mark Spitz was setting record after record in the swimming events. The whole nation was cheering him on as he won race after race. Every time he dove into the swimming pool, he would come up with another world record and another gold medal for America.

I loved the way ABC provided the television coverage. Jim McKay was the host, and the trumpets introducing the Olympics each night were great for getting you in the mood. I enjoyed those '72 Olympic Games as much as anything I had ever seen in sports.

One day, McKay interrupted the usual coverage. He looked terrible as he announced to the television audience that Arab terrorists had broken into the Olympic Village, attacked the Israeli athletes in their dormitory and were holding several of them hostage. Reports were sketchy, but it looked like people had already died.

The hours dragged on and on. Once in a while, you would get a glimpse of a hooded terrorist on the balcony of the building holding a rifle and negotiating with the police. Finally, they all got in vans and headed out to the airport. No one was sure what was going on for a while, but finally Jim McKay came on the air announcing that there had been a shoot-out at the airport and the Israeli athletes were all stuck in a couple of helicopters. The athletes had all been killed by gunfire and grenades.

I'll never forget the look on his face while he gave the news. When he finally choked out the story, he looked up into the camera and said "They're all gone."

Every once in a while that summer, I would stop in at my old employer, Soybel's Drugstore. Paul Keating's little sister, Karen, worked there. A few times, I noticed a tall, beautiful girl working in there, too. I kept asking Karen about her when I was over at the Keating's, and she told me the girl's name was Jeannie. She had just graduated from Hamden High and was going to be starting her freshman year up at UCONN. Karen didn't think she was going out with anybody, so I asked her to see if she might be interested in going to the movies with me. A couple of days later, she got back to me with the good news. Jeannie was very interested and hoped that I would call her.

I did that night, and we made plans to go out. For our first date, we went down to New Haven to the York Square Cinema to see Woody Allen in *Play It Again, Sam.* It was one of the funniest movies I had ever seen in my life. We had a great time that night laughing and really enjoying the movie. We got along great and continued seeing each other almost every night after that.

Unfortunately, the summer was winding down. I was really mad that I had not met her back in June. It would have made a great summer even more special. We only had a few weeks together before she had to get ready to leave Hamden and go up to UCONN.

September came too quickly. The wonderful summer of 1972 came to an abrupt end. Broadcasting School didn't start until October, and everyone else was heading back to college. It was the strangest sensation. I was all by myself. Everyone was gone, getting on with their lives. I was sitting at home and it all hit me like a ton of bricks. I had no idea if I was doing the right thing. I wanted to be back at college badly, and this time I would have taken it seriously. But it was too late for that. The die had been cast.

Epilogue

roadcasting school went pretty well. I could tell I was one of the better students in the class, but started to feel a little apprehensive about making a career out of radio. It seemed that most of my peers were just rock and roll star "wanna-bes." I finished among the top of the class but wasn't anxious to complete an audition tape and begin marketing myself to potential employers.

1973 was without a doubt the worst year of my life. I was now working full-time at the Knights of Columbus Printing Plant, with no idea what I wanted to do with my life. Most of my friends were still in college or beginning serious careers. I was clearly a failure at the tender age of 20, totally unfocused and lost. The best way to describe it was that it was like being in a race. Everyone else was moving forward at various speeds, yet I was half asleep at the starting line, not being able to begin. I didn't even know what direction to run in, and as each day passed, I knew I was further and further behind.

WAVZ, the New Haven radio station I had listened to so often, called me in October. It had a job opening for a person in the middle of the night. The Broadcasting School had furnished radio stations with the names of some recent graduates, and I was offered the job after an interview.

My career lasted about a year when I finally decided that radio was not the life I wanted. Disc jockeys seemed to come and go every few months, moving from Albany to New Haven to Detroit, always trying to make it big in a larger market. They would move around like gypsies. That wasn't for me.

I did, however, get more than I hoped for in that job. Working all alone in that station at 2:00 a.m., I had to be responsible, I had to be organized, I had to be punctual and I had to make decisions. I was able to do it all. The weekly salary was tiny, but the increase in my confidence and self esteem was enormous.

In 1974, I began going back to a local college at night. It's funny how when Mom and Dad had paid for all my tuition at Manhattan, I got Ds and Fs. Yet when I was paying it all myself, I got As and Bs. Somehow that college degree was no longer a goal that seemed unreachable. Maybe other things could be achieved, too.

A year later I took a job with American National Bank in Hamden as a teller, only a hundred dollars a week but a wonderful position for someone like me. How I loved that job! I was good at it, and the managers treated me like I was going places. I began doubling up on my college courses at night and took banking courses as well.

In the meantime, I had met Kathy Sweeney a year earlier and we became engaged with a wedding date of September, 1976. My life was quickly becoming better and better. 1973 now seemed like a million years ago.

One day in the spring of 1976, I was cashing a check for a man named Ken Harlan. He worked for Kemper Insurance Company around the corner, and asked me if I would ever consider a career change. There was an opening in his underwriting department and though he apologized for discussing it with me right over the counter, he thought I'd be perfect for the job. He gave me his card.

That night I discussed the day's events with my father. I loved the bank and felt I could enjoy a good career there. Dad suggested I at least explore the new opportunity since Kemper was a big company with a solid reputation. Also, we recognized that the salaries of bankers were normally less than other professions. Since I was getting married in a few months, this was an important factor.

Over the next couple of weeks I met with Mr. Harlan, his boss and his boss, too. At first it looked like my not having a college degree was going to kill my chances, but they kept giving me tests and more tests. These managers seemed to want me at Kemper. We finally made a "gentleman's agreement" that I would continue night school and get my degree, no matter how long it took. They would pay half of all the costs. I gave my word and accepted their offer of an $8,400 annual salary.

The next four years were a blur. I was now married, playing in summer softball leagues four times a week, buying our first home, learning all I could at Kemper and taking as many college courses as possible. There were many winter nights I walked across that freezing campus at Quinnipiac College, smiling and thinking how I was paying for my sins years earlier at Manhattan. However, I knew that I was simply "catching up" in a big race. It felt wonderful.

In 1980, I accepted a promotion and transfer to Springfield, Massachusetts, as the Commercial Casualty Underwriting Manager. My new boss was the Branch Manager, Herb Antine. It was here that I learned the business. Herb taught me everything he could about insurance and how to be an effective manager. He not only showed me how to be the best I could be at *my* job, but would always call me into his office to explain what he was doing in *his* job and why. Herb's interest in me, his patience and the challenges he gave me were extraordinary.

One day my mentor received the Dean of Continuing Education of American International College at his office. An hour later they called me in. There, scattered all over Herb's table, were my college transcripts and course descriptions. Somehow, Herb had talked the dean of my new college into accepting as "credits" all the things and "life-work" objectives I had achieved in insurance. I simply had to pass a few tests to verify it and pick up nine credits. Together, they also set me up for lunch hour classes each day, so I could move as quickly as possible toward my degree.

With Herb's help and encouragement, I was able to complete my end of the bargain I had made years earlier with Kemper. I finally obtained my bachelor's degree from AIC in 1982. A big promotion and transfer to Quincy, Massachusetts quickly followed. I owed so much to Herb Antine.

Meanwhile, children were being born. Bobby came in 1981 and Karen in 1983. I now had all the responsibilities of a grownup: husband, father, mortgage payments and a career. We moved back to Connecticut in late 1983 where I became involved in the Marketing Department. It was wonderful being back among family and old friends.

Early morning golf on Saturdays and Sundays at Laurel View Municipal Golf Course became my obsession. There was nothing better than standing under the stars with Roy, Tyler and Danny, drinking a cup of coffee at 5:30 a.m., waiting for the first hint of dawn to appear so we could tee off. I never played a game I enjoyed more.

In October 1987, I got the break of a lifetime: I was going to be the Branch Manager of Kemper's Charlotte, North Carolina office at the age of 35. Things couldn't have fallen into place so easily and so quickly. A fun job, beautiful home, wonderful Southern climate and people, private country club and great money. I've had so many opportunities handed to me that I can't feel anything but thankful.

However, I believe I'm even more blessed in that I've always stayed a kid on the inside. I can play the grown up game quite well, but deep down I'm still the fifth Beatle. I still feel nervous and awkward in so many situations. I'm still overwhelmed when I walk into our NFL stadium. I still get a lump in my throat when I hear certain songs. I'm still wide awake at 5:00 a.m. every Saturday like a kid on Christmas morning, looking forward to golfing with the boys at the club. I still sit down ten minutes before tee time, drinking in the atmosphere and listening to all the arguments among the guys while they make their bets. And on the first green, the adrenaline is pumping so hard my putter still shakes and I feel like I'm going to throw up.

For these types of things I haven't come very far. I'm still the same. I'm still 16 years old. I'm so lucky.